Editors
Paul Gardner
Charles Payne

Editor-in-Chief
Sharon Coan, M.S. Ed.

Art Director
CJae Froshay

Production Manager
Phil Garcia

Imaging
Ralph Olmedo, Jr.
James Edward Grace

Trademarks
Trademarked names and graphics appear throughout this book. Instead of listing every firm and entity which owns the trademarks or inserting a trademark symbol with each mention of a trademarked name, the publisher avers that it is using the names and graphics only for editorial purposes and to the benefit of the trademarked owner with no intention of infringing upon that trademark.

Publishers
Rachelle Cracchiolo, M.S. Ed.
Mary Dupuy Smith, M.S. Ed.

Be

Developing

Web Pages

for

School and Classroom

Author

Kathy Schrock

Teacher Created Materials, Inc.
6421 Industry Way
Westminster, CA 92683
ISBN-0-7439-3880-1
©2003 Teacher Created Materials, Inc.
(2nd edition)
Made in U.S.A.
www.teachercreated.com
URL updates available at our Web Site

Table of Contents

Table of Contents *(cont.)*

How to Use This Book

Welcome to the exciting world of Web page creation! It is the goal of this book to give you an orderly format to follow as you and your classroom or school goes through the process of creating your first Web pages or updating your existing ones. Remember you are using an important tool for education as you make use of World Wide Web resources with your students. As of July 1998, over 13,000 schools around the world have registered their home pages with Web66. An, nowadays, many classrooms have their own Web pages. The classes who are publishing pages are excited about the feedback they receive, teachers are enthused about their students' motivation as they participate in a global activity, and parents are enthused about following along with their child's progress and classroom activities.

The benefits of joining this revolution and promoting learning will far outweigh the trials of creating your own home page. The step-by-step method included in this book of using a template and writing a Web document will alleviate your stress and make the task a snap. There are tools available that allow you to create Web pages without knowing any of the language that is underneath all Web pages, HTML. However, it is important to understand the basics, too, and that is the direction this book takes.

Part 1: *Reasons for Having a Web Page* gives you the rationale and background you need to see the powerful effects of creating a Web page for your students. As you read though it, you will learn from the experiences of other teachers who have used the Web as a motivation for their students' achievements.

Part 2: *Questions to Answer Before Beginning* outlines the questions you should ask prior to beginning the process of planning your page. Two essays are included that present food for thought as you begin to prepare for the planning process.

Part 3: *Planning Pages* helps you start the planning process and introduces concerns about copyright and the Net.

How to Use This Book *(cont.)*

Part 4: *Collecting and Organizing Information* gives a step-by-step guide for collecting and organizing the information to use in your pages. Here you will find out how to create and collect graphics and how to start writing the content for your pages.

Part 5: *Creating a Web Page* takes you through the process of making your first page by using a template. There is also a section dealing with Web editing programs and online tools for creating usable Web pages.

Part 6: *HTML Codes and Tips* is an overview of Hypertext Markup Language (HTML) tags and what they will do on your page. Some easy techniques for making great-looking pages are included.

Part 7: *Showing Your Web Page to the World* contains instructions on viewing your page on a local computer and posting it to the Internet so that the world can see and use it.

You will next find a series of critical evaluation pages to use with students and bibliographic citation formats for use with students of all levels.

Finally, you will find a complete glossary. If at any time the language becomes confusing, visit the glossary for user-friendly definitions and explanations.

Now it is time to join in on all the excitement and write a Web page for your school and/or classroom. Enjoy the journey!

1 Reasons for Having a Web Page

Part 1: Reasons for Having a Web Page

Helping Students Focus on and Evaluate Information

Directed student use of the Internet begins to open the eyes of students as they seek current information. Many schools cannot afford daily newspapers, but the news is now online and updated often. Finding information on current topics is easier than ever. Access to information is no longer limited by the budget of the school library media center. Periodicals, newspapers, speeches, historical documents and more are at the students' fingertips. Now the focus of the class becomes how to deal with all the information. Reading comprehension becomes a necessary skill, as well as an evaluation tool to judge the quality and accuracy of the information gathered.

Paul Gilster, in his book *Digital Literacy*, makes a strong case for teaching the skills needed to utilize the new technologies. He defines digital literacy as

> the ability to understand and use information in multiple formats from a wide range of sources when it is presented via computers...Not only must you acquire the skill of finding things, you must also acquire the ability to use these things in your life. (Gilster, 1997, pp. 1 and 2)

Educators and students should not trust that what they read on the Internet is true and correct without learning some ways to critically evaluate the information. Many resources published on the Web are not seen by a publisher or evaluated by an expert before they appear. Instruction in evaluation skills and processes will prove invaluable as students are inundated with information.

1 Reasons for Having a Web Page

Snapshot from a Classroom

An example of a confusing or distracting posting appeared during the last presidential race. Many bogus pages were posted about each candidate. At times it was very difficult to know which facts were authentic. The reader of such pages had to use a critical eye to evaluate the source of the material. Often it was hard to find the name of a source or identify the author of the page.

Some articles are opinion papers, and students must begin to evaluate the references and examples used to sway the reader. They will look at the research techniques, sizes of samples, and kinds of survey questions and then decide for themselves the validity of the information. Since the materials have appeared in print, we tend to consider the information valid. Now with easy access to published and broadcast information, the need to be critical readers and use evaluation tools becomes a critical skill for survival.

1   Reasons for Having a Web Page

Helping Teachers Focus on and Evaluate Information

Before teachers can effectively train students to critically evaluate information, they have to feel comfortable with the process themselves. Pages 10 and 11 are a series of questions taken from my book *Evaluating Internet Web Sites: An Educator's Guide.* These questions begin to guide the teacher through the process of learning how to evaluate a Web page for authenticity, authority, and applicability to purpose. A series of questions for teachers to use with primary, middle, and secondary students for critically evaluating Web pages may be found on pages 214–215. An articled I authored entitled "The ABC's of Web Site Evaluation" provides a more in-depth overview of the things you and students need to think about. (**http://www.teachercreated.com/books/3880**)

In the elementary grades, most educators feel searching takes too much valuable learning time and may lead to inappropriate materials for young students. Many resource lists are available to help teachers find rich materials which can be added to a classroom home page for easy access as the students go online. Students can still evaluate the materials, but they are not overwhelmed with the quantity of information which is presented, thus leaving time to sort through the facts and support their learning.

As the students enter the intermediate grades, they will learn about the search capabilities available and be introduced to this new skill. Students should never be allowed to have free and unsupervised time on the Internet while they are at school. Students in the middle school become familiar with the search tools quickly as they seek their own information, but hopefully, by this time, they have developed strong evaluative skills and can use their time appropriately. When you begin to develop a home page with your class and want to include units of study, you will find that adding links to suggested sites and guiding students to many valuable resources is easy. These links can be changed and added as the need arises and the classroom time on the Internet is used more constructively.

1 Reasons for Having a Web Page

Tom March and Bernie Dodge at San Diego State University have categorized a number of ways of assembling resources and achieving learning with the Internet. These strategies are outlined below, and are discussed in detail on their site, *Learning with the Web* (**http://www.teachercreated.com/books/3880**)

Hotlist: Provide links to useful Web sites for your students.

Multimedia Scrapbook: Provide Internet links to photographs, maps, videos, sound files, stories, facts, quotations, insights, etc.

Treasure Hunt: Pose key questions about a topic and provide interesting Web resources that hold the answers.

Subject Sampler: Learners are presented with a smaller variety of intriguing Web sites organized around a main topic and are asked to respond to the Web-based activities from a personal perspective.

WebQuest: Present student groups with a challenging task, scenario, or a problem to solve. Provide students with all the resources they need to explore and make sense of the issues involved in the challenge. The students conclude by synthesizing their learning in a summarizing act such as e–mailing key people or presenting their interpretation to real-world experts on the topic. (March, 2001)

Students are not allowed to spend vast amounts of time in the library media center without a library media specialist making suggestions and giving guidance. The same is true as students begin to use the Internet. Many guidelines need to be in place, and giving links to specific resources can supply a student with sufficient means to evaluate without losing time searching. Adding resources and building tutorials on your Web pages will help to focus your students' work and yield the results you desire.

1 Reasons for Having a Web Page

Critical Evaluation Guide for Teachers

RATING OF WEB SITES by Kathleen Schrock (kathy@kathyschrock.net (c)1996-2002

URL: _____

SITE NAME: _____

TECHNICAL & DESIGN ASPECTS	Y	N	N/A
1. Does the Web page extend beyond the side edges of the monitor?			
2. Does the web page require extensive downward scrolling to read the information?			
3. Are there useful headings and subheadings on the page?			
4. Does the page contain graphics?			
• 4a If so, do they support the information presented on the site?			
• 4b If so, are they appropriately sized for loading at 14.400 kbps or better?			
5. When graphics are turned off, are there text alternatives?			
6. Are the grammar and spelling on the page correct?			
7. Do icons clearly represent what is intended?			
8. Is the type large enough for use by someone who is vision impaired?			
9. Can the site be used via a text-based browser?			
10. Does the site adhere to conventional HTML 2.0/3.0 rules?			
11. Is multimedia appropriately incorporated?			
12. Can the site be accessed reliably at any time of day?			

1 Reasons for Having a Web Page

NAVIGATION			
13. If an image map is present, are there also text alternatives?			
14. Are there links back to the home page from the supporting pages?			
15. Are name references (#) used wisely?			
16. Do external and internal links work?			
17. Is the overall site "user-friendly"?			
18. Is a search tool available for the site's content?			
19. Is the resource organized logically for its intended audience/purpose? (i.e., hierarchical, branching, etc.)			
AUTHORSHIP & AUTHORITY			
20. Is the page signed with a name and e-mail address?			
21. Is information about the author given?			
22. Is the author affiliated with a recognized institution?			
23. Does the author's affiliation appear to bias the information?			
CONTENT			
24. Is the purpose/mission of the site stated?			
25. Is the date of last update included?			
26. Has the site been revised recently?			
27. Is the information on the site factual in nature?			
28. Does the information appear to be opinion rather than fact?			
29. Does the site contain original information?			
30. Is a bibliography included of the sources/sites consulted?			
31. Does the information appear accurate (verifiable in a traditional print source)			
32. Does the site fulfill the stated purpose?			
33. Does the site contain primary source material?			
• 33a. If research, are research methodologies and results given?			
• 33b. If writings, are the entire documents included?			
34. Does the site include links to relevant outside sites?			
35. Is there a form or method of offering comments about the site included?			
36. Does the content seem to add to the existing body of knowledge about the topic?			

1 Reasons for Having a Web Page

Helping Students Publish on the Web

Classes throughout the years have searched the encyclopedia as they have tried to understand a world they have never seen. Students used dated resources and re-wrote the same information. They went through the motions and turned in their work. The teacher graded the work and finally sent the papers home. Today, this vision of research, writing, and publishing has changed. Imagine the power of publishing student work on the Web with the knowledge that peers around the world will read and evaluate the work. Students realize very quickly there is a reason to research carefully, write, rewrite, and edit a piece of writing. Students often surprise themselves as they are motivated to learn new information, evaluate resources, and summarize facts in many forms. The entire climate of a class changes with the prospect of publishing or posting a page on the Internet. Students can now be thought of as an important part of the academic community.

Students see themselves as a part of the research community. Publishing their work on a classroom or school Web page validates this feeling. These published reports should have links and citations for the resources the students used to research the information for the report.

Teach students to "give back to the Net." Encourage them to develop content-rich home pages focusing on something unique to their locale or interests. Increasing the number of content-rich home pages on the Web increases the depth and breadth of the information available for all. Review the slide show entitled "Creating a Content-Rich Home Page for Your School" on my Kathy Schrock's Guide for Educators slide show page.

http://www.teachercreated.com/books/3880

Your students will gain some insight as to the type of material they might include on their Web pages. For example, when publishing a report about U.S. history, students might link their reports to primary resources like those shown on the following page.

My Internet Bibliography

Original Documents

Civil War letters with real experiences of soldiers
http://www.teachercreated.com/books/3880

Declaration of Independence with some of the early, not adopted versions
http://www.teachercreated.com/books/3880

Field Trips to Historic Sites

Mount Vernon, home of George Washington Enjoy the tour, resources and ask questions of a historian.
http://www.teachercreated.com/books/3880

Colonial Williamsburg, a historical almanac where students can meet the people (including colonial children), see places, and learn interesting information about the times
http://www.teachercreated.com/books/3880

America's Home Page Plymouth, MA
http://www.teachercreated.com/books/3880

The Betsy Ross House
http://www.teachercreated.com/books/3880

Students are motivated to improve the final product and willing to go through the process it takes to get there when they know they have a purpose for writing. When writing is posted and draws comments from the readers, students become excited about beginning the next project. As Lucy Caulkins, an author of many books on process writing, once said in a workshop in Tucson, "When you publish you become a member of the club." She had been praising the use of the writing process with students and explaining she never worried much about the publishing end of the product. It was always the learning part of the process which was most important to her. However, after publishing her first book, she was struck with the power of the feeling that she was truly an author!

Giving your students this feeling creates writers in your classrooms. One way to accomplish this goal is to post their best works for a broad audience to read. This puts the focus on the published work and validates all the effort needed to create a high quality piece of writing.

Highland Park Elementary School: Student Work

http://www.teachercreated.com/books/3880

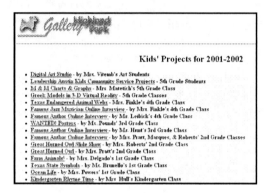

Highland Park Elementary School in Austin, Texas, has taken the work of students and posted it to share with the community. They have listed many choices of student work which can be visited.

Native American Studies

http://www.teachercreated.com/books/3880

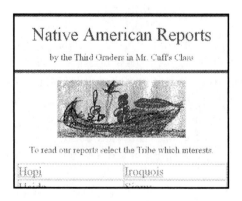

1   Reasons for Having a Web Page

One third grade completed a unit of study on Native American tribes. Each student was required to select one tribe and research information about it.

They completed the assignment by writing reports about the tribes they found interesting. Students were additionally motivated to do good jobs when they learned that the reports would be typed and posted on the school's Web pages. All students went through the writing process and were excited about seeing the results of many days of hard work. Students are now begging to be published on the Web, and a bonus use of these pages is that teachers can now show the student work as they conference with parents. This teacher was able to pull up the reports as he showed other work in the student portfolios during a recent Student-Parent-Teacher conference.

Schools are beginning to recognize that their own students are creating new resources and have begun to organize the information so it can be more easily accessed. After the tribe reports were posted, one of the teachers reported that her grandchild in another school was searching the Internet for information about American Indians and found the third grade reports. He used the information that the students had written and referenced it in his report. He received an A on his project. When this story was shared with the students who had written the reports, they began to realize that they were now the experts. They also discussed the importance of being correct with all their facts when posting a report.

1 Reasons for Having a Web Page

Mrs. Passetto's Home Page: Student Web Folios
http://www.teachercreated.com/books/3880

Many teachers now post students' original, creative work on the Net, and Ginny Passetto does this in an area she calls "Our Special Place in Great Outer-Web-Space." She shares her fourth graders' poems and other work in a consistent and appealing manner, which surely makes the students proud to have their work posted on the Web. This is her first step in creating online portfolios, or Web folios, of student work.

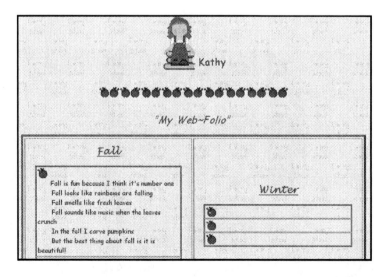

1   Reasons for Having a Web Page

Helping Teachers Publish on the Web

Using the Internet has given teachers the opportunity to publish. Many educators are creating resource lists to help teachers find the Internet resources they need. These pages are created by teachers and for teachers in an attempt to make using the Internet a more user-friendly experience. Feedback from visitors leads to rethinking some of the information posted and extensive redesign of the pages. As with any Web page, these sites are fluid creations which are always under construction.

Kathy Schrock's Guide for Educators
http://www.teachercreated.com/books/3880

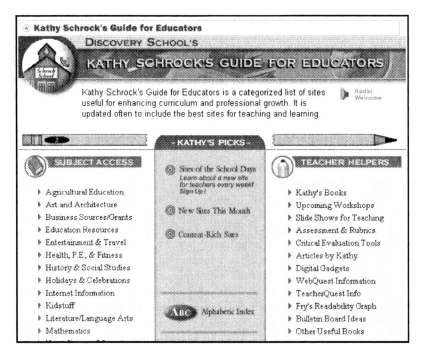

My site, on the Web since 1995, includes an annotated, classified list of over 2500 Internet links to help educators enhance the curriculum and expand their professional growth. It is global in scope and also contains original content dealing with search strategies, content-rich home pages, and critical evaluation of Web sites. As a former library media specialist and now a district technology administrator, I still continue to expand the site daily.

1 Reasons for Having a Web Page

Hazel's Homepage
http://www.teachercreated.com/books/3880

Hazel is a motivated teacher who shares her expertise with educators around the world by publishing a resource page.

This site includes the following:

- special sites for study during each month
- projects to join
- links to valuable resources
- links to keypals
- information on video conferencing

One feature of her page, the Guest Book, helps to link educators with similar interests. Anyone can view the names, e–mail addresses, and URLs of the visitors. When visiting this page, register yourself and then look at the variety of locations and personal resources which are available on the Guest Book list.

Her experience as a teacher shines through as she presents topics which can easily be integrated into current units of study. This site is a "must visit."

1 Reasons for Having a Web Page

Midge Frazel's Home Page
http://www.teachercreated.com/books/3880

This site, created by a former computer lab teacher turned educational technology trainer, contains a wealth of information to support the use of the Internet in your classroom. Some of the items include:

- Support pages for workshops ranging from locating and evaluating information to patriotism and character education are included.

- Thematic resources pages on monarch butterflies, Harry Potter, and much more.

- Resources for Web page creation, genealogy research, and free stuff on the Web for teachers.

- Information on eBooks, the Thanksgiving, and seasonal connections, as well as other links of interest to the classroom teacher.

1   Reasons for Having a Web Page

Helping Create Teachable Moments

Using the Internet as a resource is changing the way teachers plan lessons and students view their access to a world of resources. Internet resources can now supplement and complement the materials that are found in your school's library media center. You can easily access information from around the globe and bring it into your classroom on a computer screen or print it out for all to read. Working with the library media specialist in your school and planning both print and Internet resource lessons can result in a rewarding learning experience for students.

The Internet is so much more than an electronic library with static facts and millions of documents. The resources are more plentiful and content-rich than could have been imagined only a few years ago. As real-time audio and video begin to fill Web pages, students can be enchanted with speeches from the past and see events from history re-created before their eyes. Primary resources are coming out of vaults and attics and appearing for the world to read. New information is flooding onto the Web for all of us to evaluate and assimilate. This rush to publish and share seems to be unending and a little overwhelming. Current events are studied from morning papers all over the world, and access to experts of all ages leads students to think of research in a different way. As teachers see the excitement in their students, they can take advantage of the opportunities for teaching. Educators refer to a "teachable moment" as one of those times they just have to go with their feelings and take the time to teach what the students want to learn at the time they want to learn it. Teachable moments are numerous as students are exposed to these exciting resources. Teachers must learn to be flexible and take advantage of the opportunities for teaching which turn up at the most unexpected junctures. Many of these opportunities lead easily to publishing student work and adding to the information available for others.

1   Reasons for Having a Web Page

Snapshot from a Classroom

In the spring of 1995, a third grade class was introduced to using the Internet and visiting gardens around the world. This class was studying desert plants and wildlife. They were viewing gardens around the world to find information in order to compare other plants with the ones found in the desert. The one computer in the class became a center for small groups of students to use in the way that they used all the other activity centers in the classroom. Botanical gardens in several parts of the world were bookmarked, and although the resources at that time were limited, many sites on this particular topic were available.

One day students began discussing the fact that they were not seeing any cactuses in these gardens. A discussion followed, and the teacher suggested that the class write a Web page and share some information so other classes could learn about desert plants. A field trip was planned to the Desert Botanical Gardens which would prove to be a perfect project to celebrate all that the students had learned and to help with their Web page.

The class enthusiastically embraced the idea of writing reports on the plants and found their research at the garden, their picture-taking, and the writing of reports took on a strong focus. Students began to realize this information was not just an assignment to be turned into the teacher, but it was going to be read by people around the world.

1 Reasons for Having a Web Page

Tour of the Botanical Gardens
http://www.teachercreated.com/books/3880

Welcome to the Carminati third grade tour of the Desert Botanical Gardens.

In March of 1995, the classes of Mrs. Patty Chan and Mrs. Kathy Smith traveled to the Botanical Gardens. It was a glorious day and many of the desert plants were in bloom.

The following pages and reports were written by students and posted for everyone to read and enjoy. They are filled with facts about the plants found in the Sonoran Desert. We hope you enjoy your virtual tour of the Desert Botanical Garden.

Students were highly motivated as they took notes at the garden, compiled their information, completed additional research, and wrote out their reports. Students who had never before been willing to listen to advice about their writing eagerly edited their work to make the writing better. The end reports are prime examples of well-constructed third grade writing, and they are much improved over what the students would have been satisfied with if this work was not to be shown to a broader audience.

Students began to learn about writing for an audience. They discussed the need to explain their topic in clear language and include complete details. They worked hard to include correct information and use descriptive language. After considerable review, the articles were complete, and the students were proud of their final product.

1 Reasons for Having a Web Page

This class was excited about the ability they possessed to become the experts and share their knowledge about desert plants with others. They took the learning seriously because it had a purpose they could understand, and it was real. This was an extended teaching time. The teacher took the pictures of the plants they had selected and scanned them. The teacher typed the reports and then created her first classroom Web page. She was learning as she went and was asking many questions of experts she had access to. The teacher posted questions to the newsgroups to be sure that she was doing this right and had wonderful support.

The page was posted for only five days before a message arrived by e–mail from a class in Israel who had questions about the saguaro cactus and also wanted to know if we had Joshua trees. Students found Israel on the map, replied to the questions, and realized that they were now experts about our desert. A few days later was Math-Science Night at school, and students volunteered to explain their use of the Internet and display our page for parents.

Tales from the Electronic Frontier
http://www.teachercreated.com/books/3880

This is a book which was published by WESTED, a regional learning center. This project was started with a contest to find teachers who were using the Net in many different ways to teach math and science. This desert project was one of ten stories selected to share.

1   Reasons for Having a Web Page

Helping Facilitate Telecommunications Projects

Telecommunications projects are collaborative efforts among classes over long distances. Joining a project which is posted on the Internet is a great way to learn about telecommunications projects and get your class involved in long-distance learning. Many of these activities are posted each month and can easily be joined by sending e–mail. Anyone who posts a project and takes the initiative to manage all the communications is counting on each participant to make this activity a valuable learning experience for all classes involved. If any part of the project is not completed, all classes involved in the project may be disappointed. It is important to plan carefully and follow through if your class joins a project. When a project is posted, facilitators will count on full participation from each class.

Judi Harris, in her book entitled *Virtual Architecture: Designing and Directing Curriculum-Based Telecomputing* (ISTE, 1997), classifies and annotates the various types of telecomputing activities that teachers can participate in with their classes.

Interpersonal Exchange

One of the oldest and most popular types of educational telecomputing activities is one in which individuals talk electronically with other individuals, individuals talk with groups, or groups talk with other groups. This can be accomplished using electronic mail, asynchronous large-group discussion tools (such as Web conferences or newsgroups), or in real time with text or audio-video conferencing tools (such as IRC or CU-SeeMe). There are six activity structures currently associated with interpersonal exchange processes.

Structure 1: Keypals

This was the first commonly used telecomputing activity structure, similar in form to surface mail pen pal activities. Students who are participating in activities that are formed with this structure usually are paired off to communicate with each other electronically. The topics they discuss often are suggested by the students themselves.

1 Reasons for Having a Web Page

Student-to-student keypal exchanges often involve quite a bit of managerial work for the classroom teacher to make them successful. The transfer and processing of multiple electronic mail messages sent through a single class account, or the monitoring of many messages by a single teacher if students have their own e–mail accounts to use, can make keypal activity structures difficult to justify in terms of time and effort expended.

Group-to-group exchanges (called global classrooms and presented in the next section), especially those with a particular curricular emphasis, can evolve into fascinating collaborative explorations without overwhelming the activity facilitator.

Structure 2: Global Classrooms

With this activity structure, two or more classrooms in different locations can study a common topic together during a previously specified time period. Global classroom structures are more often used than the keypal structures, probably due to the logistical difficulties explained in the last section. Also, global classroom activities seem to lend themselves better to specific content focuses and, therefore, may be perceived by teachers to fit better into the curriculum.

Structure 3: Electronic Appearances

Interpersonal exchanges can also result in the hosting of a special guest with whom students can communicate either in real time or asynchronously. Such electronic appearances are usually made on a one-time basis by someone who is a subject-matter expert. In some cases, electronic appearances are made by famous experts, such as children's authors or famous politicians.

1　Reasons for Having a Web Page

Although electronic appearances can be conducted using electronic mail or asynchronous computer conferencing tools, most are done using real-time text chat or video conferencing, such as CU-SeeMe or NetMeeting. This establishes a presence for the session's participants and accommodates the short-term nature of this kind of activity. The Global SchoolNet site includes links to this type of information. (**http://www.teachercreated.com/books/3880**)

Structure 4: Telementoring

Internet-connected subject matter specialists from universities, business, government, or other schools can serve as electronic mentors for students wanting to explore specific topics of study in an interactive format. Some projects may cost money, but others do not. An example of the types of activities may be found on the International Telementor Program site.

(**http://www.teachercreated.com/books/3880**)

Structure 5: Question-and-Answer Activities

As the amount and type of information available online grow exponentially, so can our difficulties with finding answers to questions that specifically meet our students' needs as learners. For students who either can't find the information they need to fully answer a question they have, or who don't fully understand the information they have found online, a question-and-answer activity might be appropriate. Of all of the activity structures that have emerged as the Internet is appropriated for educational use, question-and-answer activities are the briefest in duration.

Structure 6: Impersonations

Impersonation projects are those in which any (or all) of the participants communicate with each other while in character. Department of Defense Schools teachers April Vega and Bonnie Hopkinson-Johnson, for example, worked with fourth- and fifth-grade classes reading historical fiction, such as *Conrad, Pedro's Journal, A Voyage with Christopher Columbus; Speare, The Sign of the Beaver; Fritz, What's the Big Idea, Ben Franklin?; and Lenski, Indian Captive, The Story of Mary Lemison,* and helping them to communicate via e–mail as the books' protagonists. Characterizations were provided by adult members of the administrative and teaching staffs.

1   Reasons for Having a Web Page

Collection and Analysis

Some of the most successful educational telecomputing activities involve students collecting, compiling, and comparing different types of interesting information. With the advent of the World Wide Web and its wealth of available resources, this purpose for educational telecomputing has become quite popular.

Structure 7: Information Exchanges

There are many examples of thematically conceptualized information exchange that have been employed as curriculum-based telecomputing activities. Students and their teachers from all around the globe have collected, shared, compared, and discussed many types of information.

Sharing information that is intrinsically interesting to young people on an international scale is an excellent way to engage students in authentic cultural interchange. One of the best examples of curriculum-related information exchange is David Warlick's yearly Global Grocery List project in which students from all over the world collect and compare the prices for each item on a common, but virtual, shopping list.

Information exchanges can involve many classes without becoming an overwhelming managerial task for teachers. Projects such as these are particularly appropriate uses for telecomputing tools because the participating students become creators, consumers, and critics of the information they are sharing.

1 Reasons for Having a Web Page

Structure 8: Database Creation

Some information collection and analysis projects involve not only collecting but also organizing the information into databases that project participants and others can use for study. Successful information exchange activities can easily grow into database creation activities.

Structure 9: Electronic Publishing

Increasing numbers of schools with high-speed access to the Internet along with the proliferation of Web page authoring tools have made it quite easy for primary through secondary electronic publishing projects to take place. The appeal of an international audience for students' work is very powerful, so many examples of electronic publishing projects are viewable online.

Structure 10: Tele-Field Trips

Local field trips can be an engaging, beneficial educational experience for students. Yet funding constraints and geographical location may limit frequent and productive curriculum-based traditional field trip options for many schools. A very popular type of online project, the tele-field trip, can open virtual doors to field trip experiences that all students can enjoy.

This rapidly growing type of online project has two main variations. The first, and simplest to organize, involves students in one location taking a field trip locally and sharing their experiences directly with other students interested in similar curriculum-related experiences.

The second, and by far the most popular, type of tele-field trip is essentially a virtual expedition usually taken by adults who are researching scientific relationships or historical sites. Online participants are invited to experience the expedition, usually in multimedia form, via the World Wide Web and, in some cases, remotely participate in the inquiry.

1   Reasons for Having a Web Page

Structure 11: Pooled Data Analysis

Information exchanges are particularly powerful when data are collected at multiple sites and then combined for pattern analysis. The simplest of these types of activities involves students electronically issuing a survey, collecting the responses, analyzing the results, and reporting their findings to all participants.

Problem Solving

Problem solving is one of the most beneficial educational opportunities that we can offer to students of any age. The Internet can be used to support problem-based learning around the world. Problem-solving projects are, as yet, the smallest area of educational telecollaborative activity, but they are among the best examples of how connectivity can be used to support and enrich K–12 curricula.

Structure 12: Information Searches

Problem solving online can be either competitive or collaborative. In the simplest form of problem-solving activity, students are provided with clues and must use reference sources, found either online or offline, to answer questions. Information searches are usually structured as competitive activities with the winning individuals or teams being those who correctly answer the most questions by a common, short-term deadline.

Information search activities can also be of longer duration and embody rather extensive and sophisticated research, analysis, and communication activities for the participating students. Typically, educational endeavors supported with this structure include many deductive and convergent reasoning activities.

Structure 13: Peer Feedback Activities

Peer feedback activities encourage participants to offer constructive responses both to others' ideas and to the forms in which those ideas are expressed.

Structure 14: Parallel Problem Solving

Using this popular activity structure, a similar problem is presented to students in several locations. They explore the problem separately at each site, and then come together online to compare, contrast, and discuss their various problem-solving methods. Such rich and varied problem solving, accompanied by discussion of multiple problem-solving methods, is a popular project for telecollaborating classes.

Structure 15: Sequential Creations

An intriguing kind of artistic problem solving has emerged on the Internet, one in which participants progressively create either a common written text or a shared visual image. The sequential-creation activity structure seems to be applied using a variety of expressive media to support intriguing collaborative creative efforts.

Structure 16: Telepresent Problem Solving

Telepresent problem-solving activities bring together participants from different geographic locations and time zones, asynchronously or in real time, to virtually participate in a computer-mediated meeting, to use remotely located robotic tools, or to simultaneously engage, without direct electronic contact, in similar activities at different project sites.

Structure 17: Simulations

Online simulations require the most coordination and maintenance of all activities created with these activity structures; however, the depth of learning possible, and the task engagement displayed by participants, can convince project organizers to spend the additional time and effort necessary to make simulations work well.

Structure 18: Social Action Projects

It should be no surprise to global citizens living in this day and age that the Internet can serve as a context for "humanitarian, multicultural, action-oriented

1 Reasons for Having a Web Page

telecommunications projects" (Gragert,1997) that involve the future leaders of our planet. These undertakings are called social action projects because of their focus upon real and immediate problems and their orientation towards students taking action towards a resolution rather than stopping with just understanding of the problem.

The potential for multidisciplinary, forward-thinking, truly collaborative learning when involved in projects such as these is unlimited. It also is important to note that many of the more sophisticated, interdisciplinary, authentic online problem-solving projects focus their participants' attention upon the problems to solve rather than on the telecommunications technologies used to share information among distant collaborators. This clear emphasis upon curriculum-infused learning, rather than the technologies that facilitate that learning, is one of the characteristics that makes Internet-based problem-solving projects so potentially powerful. (Harris, 1997)

Planning your own project can be very rewarding, but it will require time and effort. Plan it as you would any unit activity by writing out the learning objectives first. Create a timeline for the project and list the expectations for the participants. Write up a summary of the project so it can be posted with the objectives to help other classes decide if they are interested in participating in your project. Write a letter of acceptance and a letter for those not selected to be sent as you receive the requests for participation. Be careful to limit the number of participants, especially if this is your first project. Some projects can quickly become complex to administer and overwhelming to manage. Be aware of the additional amount of time which will be required to coordinate communication among all participants. If you are planning to post the results of the participants' work, allow time to get this done.

1   Reasons for Having a Web Page

Title of project: A catchy title can be interesting, but make sure it fits in a subject line of e–mail and includes enough information to get the readers to open the posting.

Contact information: Include the name, address, phone, and e–mail address of the coordinator.

Objectives for project: List the main learning objectives so others can evaluate the benefits to their students.

Age, location, and any qualifying information of participating classes: Make sure to include the specifics on the type of students you are looking for.

Number of students or classes needed: State the number of classes or students you wish to use in the project.

Summary of project and participant responsibilities: Keep this brief for the initial posting.

Timeline of activities and dates the responses are due to be submitted: Send only the overview of the dates on the posting and include all of the information in your introductory letter to explain the details of the project.

Information about the project celebration and sharing: Sharing the results of the project is the strongest reason that someone will want to participate in your project. Make all the information available to the participating classes.

How to register for the project: Make registration easy. Sending an e–mail message with class information should be all they need to do for you to begin the process of deciding which classes to select for the project.

Response letter to accepted participants: This letter needs to include all the details of how to submit information, the format to have pictures and text ready to post on pages, and any other information to make completion of the project a shared responsibility.

1 Reasons for Having a Web Page

Response letter to those not selected: If you know that you are going to post a Web page and show the results of the project, it is nice to share the address and encourage the classes not chosen to participate to watch for postings. Keep the names and addresses of these responding classes because you may want to join with them in later projects.

Plan for ongoing communications during the project: Remember the participating classes need to hear from you on a regular basis. This communication keeps the interest high and helps to remind everyone of the timeline of activities.

Call for Participants

Once the project is planned you need to advertise it to educators who are looking for telecommunication projects to join. One good place to post the information is the HILITES mailing list. If you subscribe to this list, you will receive notices of new projects, and your project can be seen by many teachers.

To join HILITES send an e–mail message to the following address: majordomo@gsnlists.org. Type "subscribe hilites" (without quotes) in the body of the e–mail message or visit the mailing list Web page to subscribe online. **http://www.teachercreated.com/books/3880**

Global SchoolNet: Internet Projects Registry
http://www.teachercreated.com/books/3880

Posting your project to this list will automatically place the project in the Global SchoolNet Projects Registry database. It is recommended that you begin by posting in only one place so that you are not overwhelmed by the number of responses.

1   Reasons for Having a Web Page

Finding Projects to Join

Many projects are posted each month, and you can quickly learn where to look to take advantage of these creative learning activities. Some resource locations post collections of projects. The Global SchoolNet Project has a wealth of information whether you want to join the perfect activity or are just planning to design your own project and use the site to look for ideas.

Other resources for projects include the Houghton Mifflin Education Place: Project Center (**http://www.teachercreated.com/books/3880**)

Snapshot from a Classroom

The call for participation shown on the next page, "The Cyber-travels of Flat Stanley," was posted on a Friday afternoon and, by Monday morning, over fifty classes wanted to participate. The teacher printed the responses and asked her students to read them and decide which classes they wanted to accept. Students evaluated the location of each school, the enthusiasm of the note, and made their decisions. After the schools were chosen, notes had to be sent out to give details about the project. All schools that were not selected were notified that other classes were chosen, and they were given the address of a planned Web page where all the collections would be posted. They were encouraged to visit the page to see how the project was developing.

Once the project began, each classroom team was assigned two schools to keep in touch with and write to often. Any e–mail received from a school had to be answered promptly by the teams. A running commentary during the project led to better follow-through on the part of all participants and, as a bonus, new friends for the students in the classes. Students would write about projects in their classes as well as report on the many adventures of Flat Stanley.

1   Reasons for Having a Web Page

The plan for this project was to have students in many states write articles about their states. Each class put their own spin on the format. Some sent a group story about Flat Stanley traveling around their state. A creative teacher in New York State incorporated many facts about the state as she and her class wove a story together. They sent student drawings to illustrate Stanley's many adventures. You can find out more about it on this page:
http://www.teachercreated.com/books/3880

Welcome to the Cyber-travels of Flat Stanley

This collaborative project was posted by Mrs. Chan's Fourth Grade Class at Carminati Elementary. It continues to collect information about the many places where classes of children are taking their Flat Stanley.

1 Reasons for Having a Web Page

Facilitating Communication

One of the unique aspects of the Internet is that everyone is accepted based solely on what they write. It does not matter if you are ten or ninety, your opinion is as clear and as strong as the message you send. Your Web page can start a dialog just by communicating information about yourself or your classroom.

Snapshot from a Classroom

A teacher once received an e–mail from a person who had seen her home page. He complimented her on the layout of resources and then made a few suggestions of resource sites to add. At the end of his message, he shared with the teacher that he writes software reviews and these could be found on his school's home page. It was not until he told the teacher that he was ten years old that she realized she was hearing from a student. As far as the teacher was concerned, they were equals working toward a common cause.

In Kansas City, Missouri, students participated in a program in which keypals were matched up between a suburban school and an urban school. The students corresponded for most of a year, and then a trip was planned so the students could meet. Students were surprised to discover at the meeting that although they came from different cultures and lived in different environments, they shared many of the same beliefs and goals. This demonstrated a powerful way to show students that what they do and think is the great equalizer.

It is the personal contact and the mutual support that brings everyone back to the computer screen. The Internet provides a number of wonderful and unique opportunities for all its users. You may enjoy the glitzy pictures and sounds on the World Wide Web today, but it is the e–mail account that has made many dependent on the Internet. Users continue to meet interesting people with common interests and to make new friends. Most teachers enjoy working with a global community of educators. They share ideas, compare experiences, and work to enhance the use of technology in education.

1 Reasons for Having a Web Page

Snapshot from a Classroom

A prospective teacher contacted a teacher at a school with many questions. She had seen the teacher's class page and, from the page, learned that she was teaching a multi-age class. The college student sent an e–mail to the teacher with questions about working in such an environment. That long-distance conversation has continued between the United States and Australia. This opportunity for both educators to communicate and learn from each other would not have been possible without an Internet connection and the initial effort on the part of the classroom teacher to create a class page and share how she is working with her students.

The interactivity of Web pages and the use of e–mail are propelling the Internet into the classrooms of the world. Teachers and students can reach out to others for answers and support. Lives are richer, not because users have searched the Net, but because of the strangers who have become their mentors and friends. It is after you begin to support others, respond to questions, and post information that you truly receive the enormous benefits of Internet use.

E–mail allows teachers throughout a district to communicate quickly. Services and one-on-one training can be tailored to the questions asked as support personnel answer their daily e–mail messages. Prompt answers and replies with additional information can help lead to rapid learning. This quick communication facilitates continuous learning and the flow of information from all sides. E–mail can also be used within a district to send memos and newsletters rather than the traditional paper format, saving money and speeding access. All of this communication keeps teachers informed and motivates them to try new activities.

1 Reasons for Having a Web Page

Often it seems to be the accidental meeting on the Net which can prove to be most beneficial. You will find most people online are cooperative and eager to help when questions or concerns are posted. Many new to the Net begin learning about the Internet by "lurking" (visiting and observing without participating) on a newsgroup for several weeks before they answer a question or complete a survey. They are just learning the ropes from those who were there first. As you become more confident, you will post questions and find the information you need. Reading the newsgroups and learning from other educators excited about the ability of this new technology to enhance learning is an important first step to being an active citizen on the Internet, a "Netizen."

Working in a structured environment with four walls and a closed door has always kept teachers and students isolated. Teachers have had limited time to talk with colleagues to share ideas. Making a change or learning something new about their profession was usually self-motivated and self-financed. In past years, the same old ways of doing things seemed to work as classes came and went and students appeared to learn. But now, with the emphasis in education on standards, real-life assessments, and interdisciplinary lessons, teachers need to find new strategies to enhance student achievement. Educators are seeking help to enhance their teaching methods and do a better job at what they love doing—teaching.

1   Reasons for Having a Web Page

Enhancing Home-School Communication

As the public focus strengthens on a need to infuse technology into the classroom, schools are beginning to acquire the hardware and training support they have needed for years. Districts which have created a vision for improving student achievement are directing funds toward the classrooms and purchasing tools which open the walls and let classes travel the world. Schools are wiring their buildings and setting up wide area networks. Computers are appearing in classrooms, and labs are being wired. Funding for training is the most limited aspect of the process, yet it is assumed that once the hardware is in place, the teacher will use this new equipment for the benefit of students to enhance their achievement. Teachers are working doubly hard to learn about the opportunities this technology brings to enhance student learning. As teachers share their success stories, they learn from each other and develop better methods for using these powerful tools. I have written an article entitled "Creating Class Web Sites" which provides a brief overview of some of the questions, concerns, and ideas you need to have in place before you start.
(http://www.teachercreated.com/books/3880)

Schools are beginning to see the benefits of posting a Web page and publicizing the positive side of education to the community at large. They are taking advantage of this medium to display school mission statements, share information about school programs, and call for volunteers and business partners to join in and help. Each school has a personality and a culture which is unique to that situation and population. By posting a Web page with information about the school, you also are sharing the culture of that school.

An elementary school in Arizona has a business partnership with Motorola. During one school year, some of the engineers volunteered to teach rocketry to fifth grade classes. They came faithfully for several weeks to build the background knowledge about the science of rockets and jet propulsion.

1   Reasons for Having a Web Page

To extend the project, each team of students was supplied with the materials and instruction for rocket building. As this activity was happening, pictures were taken and then posted to our school page. The engineers were asked if they would mind having the information posted, and not only did they agree, they were eager to show their company what was happening at the school. The project is planned for additional years, and the staff intends to have the students write in journals after each lesson and then post some of the students' insights along with additional pictures of the work.

LAUNCH DAY

2000

Great Looking Rockets!

Feature any other projects at your school for the community to share. Math-Science Night provides a perfect opportunity to post student projects and build school pride, as well as Open House displays, science fairs, international luncheons, and the "fun" days such as Spirit Day, Hat Day, Slipper Day, etc.

1   Reasons for Having a Web Page

Families often comment on the projects and tell how they share these pages with distant grandparents. Again this is an example of how you can share with the community what is happening in your school.

Think of the activities you could share:

- assemblies
- evening performances
- science fairs
- art shows
- field trips

Open the doors of your school by posting the following:

- dates of upcoming events
- invitations to participants and volunteers
- exhibitions and student work
- results and minutes of school district meetings

Using the Internet will not solve all the ills of education today. However, it is hoped that you are beginning to see how educators can excite their students and themselves and bring rich and real learning experiences into an otherwise isolated learning environment. You can become an active participant in this new wave of technological advances. With these new technologies, teachers and students quickly understand how learning and life come together. The puzzle pieces of formal education start to fit together more easily. You are invited to begin to bring the Internet into your classroom and continue to raise your comfort level with all the new tools until you decide to join the Web by joining a project or creating a school or class Web page.

Part 2: Questions to Answer Before Beginning

School Home Page Questions

First, let's focus on the school home page and whether it is the next technology step for you and your school. Technology committees around the country are meeting to decide whether their schools should post a home page and what type of information should be included. They commonly debate the technical questions first, such as who will write and maintain it, where it should be housed, who will be writing the text and doing the planning, and what graphics should be included.

The more important questions which should probably be discussed first include the following:

What benefits can our school gain from having a home page?

What image do we want to present to the community?

How can a presence on the World Wide Web enhance student achievement?

What benefits can your school gain from having a home page?

With the posting of a school home page, your school joins thousands of schools who are sharing their successes with the global community. Most schools are public institutions which must be accountable to the community for what they are doing. What better way to report to the community than to post an extensive Web page which opens the school's doors and welcomes anyone in to look around.

2 Questions to Answer Before Beginning

Web66

http://www.teachercreated.com/books/3880

 Web66: International School Web Site Registry

Web66 is the location of the most extensive listing of schools around the world with Web pages.

Below you can see a partial listing, illustrating how international in scope this list really is!

International Schools

Elementary Schools 119

1. Academy International Elementary Colorado Springs, Colorado USA
2. Academy Ste Cecile International School Windsor, Ontario Canada
3. American International School of Manila Manila, Philippines
4. Ambrit Rome International School Rome, Italy
5. American - Nicaraguan School Managua, Nicaragua
6. American Collegiate Institute Ozel Izmir American Lisesi Izmir, Turkey
7. American Community School Amman, Jordan
8. American Community School of Abu Dhabi Abu Dhabi, United Arab Emirates
9. American Cooperative School of Tunis Tunis, Tunisia
10. American Institute of Monterrey Monterrey, Mexico
11. The American International School of Johannesburg Johannesburg, South Africa
12. American International School Vienna Vienna, Austria
13. American Overseas School of Rome Rome, Italy
14. The American School Mexico City, Mexico
15. American School in Japan Chofu, Tokyo Japan
16. American School of Bucharest Bucharest, Romania
17. American School of Guadalajara Guadalajara, Mexico
18. American School of Tegucigalpa Tegucigalpa, Honduras

The community should know about the great things that are happening in their schools. To promote more positive feelings towards education, one powerful way to change public opinion is to open the doors and invite the public in to your classes. Learning is going on in each and every class, and many classes are exceptional. These experiences must be available to the public and shared with others in the educational community. Educators need to sing their own praises and display high quality student work for the world to view.

2 Questions to Answer Before Beginning

For decades, businesses have used advertising and public relations experts to promote their products and establish themselves as pillars of the community. They have built intangible assets which pay off in goodwill toward the company as well as increased sales. The time has come for schools to engage in this same process and do a little self-promotion. Having intangible assets will pay off big when the next bond issue comes to a vote or the legislature wants to cut the educational budget. Often, all the public knows about the schools in their community is what they read in the newspapers. Now the schools have a tool which allows them to publish their own stories. They can focus on the learning activities, student accomplishments, and educational success stories.

Think about sharing the story of the student who tutors a younger child, the teacher who always stays late to help students, and the principal who continually writes grants to try to fund school projects. All of these and many more small, positive events happen each day, and the community needs to know. They need to visit your school or class home page and understand learning is a team effort and the school team is making significant progress. Make good use of this new, effective voice which comes to your school because you have access to the World Wide Web.

Many people would not even consider visiting the school or spending a day in the classrooms, but they might click on a few buttons and open a Web page which gives them a virtual tour through the hallways and classrooms of your school. The focus of your school Web site should be carefully crafted so all visitors feel welcome and can easily travel through the information as well as contact the school with follow-up questions.

A school home page can enhance school pride and begin to make teachers and students aware of why their school is so special. A feeling of school spirit should jump off the pages and entice others to join in the learning process. If your school is looking for volunteer tutors, parents to help with projects in classes, or the donation of computers to enhance a science center, these issues can be addressed on your page.

2   Questions to Answer Before Beginning

Many school pages post the following:

- current calendars of events for easier planning
- dates of school holidays
- parent conference times with e–mail access to send notes to the teacher
- times and locations of performances
- sporting events, locations, times, past records and scores
- locations for field trips and even copies of the permission forms which parents can print and sign if they have been lost
- online school lunch menus which might help to make the decision about bringing or buying lunch during that rushed morning at home

On the more professional side, you can also post these items:

- mission statements
- action plans for school improvement
- school committees and member lists
- solicitations for volunteers
- school committee (or board) minutes
- resource links to curriculum materials
- class pages with student work
- staff information and e–mail addresses
- job openings, volunteer or paid
- applications for employment
- school statistics, class sizes, length of periods
- special class schedules for music, PE, band
- student portfolios of class work
- monthly newsletter from the superintendent

2 Questions to Answer Before Beginning

Some school pages also include numerous Internet-based resource links for the teachers to use as they plan their lessons or units. These links help everyone at the school use the Net more efficiently and set up bookmarks for future student use. The school page can be the link to many resources which everyone can check often, and can easily tie in Web use to the content standards.

As you begin to see the benefits of designing and posting a school page, take all these ideas and use the ones which are right for you and your situation. The home page must reflect the school and your plans for the future to be effective and useful for your staff and community.

What image do you want to present to the community?

Consider what the community thinks it knows about your school and then consider what else you want them to know. How can your school Web page help to develop an image of the school as you see it? This image might prove to be a self-fulfilling prophecy as you take your staff's vision of the school and portray it on the school home page. In order to have the material to post to substantiate your claims, the classes have to continue to complete the outstanding projects, write the detailed reports, participate in the hands-on learning events, and reach out to the community with activities. Fulfilling a vision is tough, but if you don't have the vision first, you will never initiate the change needed to reach that goal. The school home page can become the showcase of the changes and a motivator for all the staff to continue to work for improvement and success.

Education is often the minds of the taxpayers these days. School populations are growing and the buildings are often crowded, and more schools have to be built each year. With the increase in students entering the system, the costs escalate exponentially. Society is redefining the role of the school, and this definition seems to include much more than the three R's. If your school offers additional services, extended hours, a year-round schedule, or other special services for the students and the community, these should be shared on your school home page.

2 Questions to Answer Before Beginning

Don't worry about the graphics and the look of the home page until you have the main ideas down on paper. Think seriously about this issue; discuss it in meetings and with your active parent community. Make a plan and then know it can always be changed. Think of the many focuses you can take and remember the one you select should reflect the culture of your school. This process may take some time and many serious discussions, but it will pay off in the final product. As with most things, this careful planning will be evident in the final Web site.

How can a presence on the World Wide Web enhance student achievement?

Since providing students with an education is the reason for schools, remember to think about the development of a school Web page that will positively affect student learning. In addition to including the content areas for students, emphasize some of the information literacy process skills, such as searching and evaluation or Web pages as well as the ethics of computer use. The content area standards should be infused with these technology process skills which will be necessary for students to be able to work well and compete in an information-rich environment.

The creation of a school home page can enhance student desire to read and write as they participate in class projects, write surveys, compile information, write reports, project results, and calculate information. Technical skills will begin to emerge, as well. Students at the middle school and high school levels can be the administrators of the network, set up new computers, add network cards to existing machines, and assist the district in bringing more computers online. These students can also assist in the writing of comprehensive Web pages. Schools are finding that these skills can be learned quickly by students and transferred easily to the business world.

2   Questions to Answer Before Beginning

Some business partners are eager to come into the school and train "local experts" to assist the school as technical challenges arise. Many students are often involved in school-based technology and some high schools even offer training for computer certifications as part of the curriculum. The scenario illustrated in the following note is not atypical of the support students often provide in the schools.

Date: Sat, 28 Dec 2002 16:30:58-0800 (PST)

From: Joe Stewart <stewartj@hotmail1.com>

Subject: student system administrators story

I have two Windows 2000 Server administrators for both faculty accounts and student accounts. In each case these are upperclass students I have worked with for several years each. We tend to be more like collaborators rather than having the typical teacher-student relationship. Several other students take care of software and hardware problems and the usual troubleshooting that can take place on any given day. In general, students spend one period per day with me, but during my absence several of them have spent many extra hours. The feedback from administrators, faculty, district tech people, and others has been pretty fantastic in their praise for the work of these kids and their abilities to keep our system up and running.

The issue of school tech support has always been a difficult one for many school districts to handle. From my experience, it appears that there is some room for student participation in the overall scheme of tech support, given good preparation and attention to ethics, responsibilities, and character. I hope to write a more complete account of this process in the near future and hope that others of you can contribute your good news stories as well.

Joe Stewart

stewartj@hotmail1.com

---

2   Questions to Answer Before Beginning

Many high school students are major players in the technical creation of their school's home page. Their knowledge of the newest technologies, such as Flash and ASP.net, allow for exciting, interactive Web pages to be produced.

The basic skills of creating the Web pages, submitting them to an advisor for approval, and then posting them to a server can be easily learned by students. If the facilities are available and class time is allotted, students rapidly pick up these skills. Using this time for technical learning soon becomes a curriculum question for the school. How much time can a student spend with technology? Do these alternative skills fulfill state and national standards? These questions are being addressed at the present time.

Technology standards have been developed which include many of the skills students are eager to learn. Watch closely as the world begins to realize that more life skills and, specifically, technology skills as outlined in the various technology standards should be included in the school curriculum.

Links to both the National Educational Technology Standards for Students (NETS*S) and McREL's Technology Standards may be found on **http://www.teachercreated.com/books/3880**

Your school home page can be a catalyst for changes in instruction and attitude among your staff and students. Be careful to focus on learning and what the result will be as you plan your school home page. Focus all projects and correspondence from a school home page on the curriculum, and you will find that the Internet becomes a tool which enhances and enriches student learning.

2 Questions to Answer Before Beginning

Snapshot from a Classroom

The home page for our school was designed and presented to us by a graduate student who was working with the school to help all staff understand the Internet and troubleshoot all the technical challenges. He created the page and brought it to the technology team for approval. At that time, we did not know much about the impact of school home pages and were thrilled to have our school name posted on the Web. Our elementary school was the first in Arizona to post a page, and that was exciting too.

What we did see after posting the page was it provided an avenue to showcase our creative classroom projects and exceptional student work. The possibility of posting information under the school banner motivated the staff to follow through with projects and then find parent volunteers to type the information so that it could be posted. Everyone got caught up in the excitement! Student writing was posted by many classes, and the quality of the work selected motivated others to work harder to qualify to have their pieces of writing shared.

Teachers asked students to describe projects and class activities as they involved them in the design and presentation of class home pages.

Educators and global community members began reading the school page regularly and checking for changes and additions. Comments poured in and motivated more activity. All of this excitement was generated over a period of years, and it has only intensified a feeling of school spirit.

2 Questions to Answer Before Beginning

More class projects are planned for the future. Our teachers were already doing the interactive projects with their students and integrating many resources into their thematic units. Now that they can showcase their work and receive comments, they are receiving the well-deserved rewards of hard work.

The other area of achievement which was affected was the easy access to references for research. Links were provided on the home page to directly connect students and teachers to the resources they needed. There was no need for everyone to search for resources or set up individual bookmarks. As class home pages were added, many of the often-used links were available at the click of an icon.

Because of the communications which were opened by the presence of our school page on the Web, classrooms conducting class projects easily found partner schools, and our school posted the activity results. Many of the schools who were most interested in participating had no access to a server on the Internet and could not post their student work locally. They were pleased to have us include their work.

As the questions poured in, our staff found themselves involved in teacher mentoring. They corresponded with educators around the world about topics from our year-round schedule, multi-age classrooms, and organization of student projects to questions about using our computers. Many questions have come in about our hardware setup, and most are surprised by the limitations of our hardware because of the quantity and quality of our postings. Being less than a mile south of Arizona State University, and partnering with the university as often as possible, has helped our students. This cooperative action has led to numbers of university technology interns working with classes to enhance the achievement of our students, train our staff in new technology skills, and gain many practical benefits for themselves.

We find that learning together makes it possible to reach the high goals we set for ourselves. With this and other continued support, our staff anticipates change and is much more accepting of new ideas that come with it. Although, like everyone, they sometimes feel overwhelmed with the newness of each task, they are confident enough to let the students lead when they have skills needed by the classroom teacher. Staff members have also attended classes and learned computer skills they can incorporate into their future lessons. These teachers have become local experts and now can mentor others on staff.

Susan Hixson, Tempe (AZ) Public Schools

2 Questions to Answer Before Beginning

Investigate any local institutions which might be interested in sending interns to work with your staff. Web projects take additional time to coordinate and post, and extra hands are most helpful with this task. If you have active parent volunteers, you may want to set up training sessions so they can also become involved with the home page production. Parents and other volunteers can quickly be trained to scan pictures and save them to the server. Extra hands really help with the many steps to writing and posting Web pages.

Many elementary schools do not introduce Web page creation to their students. Of course, this is partially determined by the student access to computers and the structure of the curriculum. Until the students have access to more computers, taking time to create pages is probably not the best use of the one computer in the classroom. However, students should be aware of what the HTML page looks like "behind" their displayed work. This can easily been accomplished by having them choose "View Source" from the browser menu. Many of the current tools used with students, such as *Inspiration, AppleWorks, Microsoft Publisher,* and *Microsoft Word* now allow students to create a Web page by simply choosing "save as a Web page" from the menu. This an easy way for elementary students to create Web pages without learning HTML.

As you design and post a school home page, you will begin to see the many ways in which student achievement is positively impacted. It will be your responsibility to try creative uses of this new method of display and to monitor and test the benefits. Share your success stories by writing articles and presenting at conferences. Educators must help each other to infuse use of the Internet into all areas of the curriculum, and what you learn and share can be just the catalyst to help and motivate someone else.

2 Questions to Answer Before Beginning

Class and Project Home Page Questions

A class home page can be thought of as an electronic home where your students are guided to appropriate sites and information from many resources. Decorate that home page with "windows" which let the students peer out to find exciting resources and visit with neighbors near and far. Provide doors which open wide to visitors who bring different experiences, cultures, and new ideas to consider. You will want to create an image of your class for the world to see which represents the "home" of your classroom. Join the growing number of teachers who are writing home pages and contributing to the resources on the Internet. By adding your influence to the world of technology, you encourage students to make a connection between the activities in today's class and those in tomorrow's world of work.

As you decide whether you want to venture into the realm of home page development with your class, there are some questions to discuss.

Is the benefit of writing a home page worth the effort?

How does having a home page help to infuse new resources into the required curriculum?

Is the benefit of writing a home page worth the effort?

You will be amazed at the many responses you receive as people from around the world come across your page. The benefits are many as your students hear from experts. A fourth grade class received e–mail from a scientist who had recently returned from Antarctica. He read work posted by this class and was writing to volunteer to answer any questions the class might have for him. This response to a class page led to a rich resource for that class, and the scientist also helped a novice second grade teacher make the study of Antarctica come to life for her students.

2 Questions to Answer Before Beginning

School and class pages often are filled with student work and smiling faces. The powerful ones have their own distinct personalities because of their uses of colors and graphics and methods of presentation. This illustrates that the school has many divergent thinkers who all come together to make a special place for learning. Teachers are making choices as they decide to join in the fun of using the Internet to promote education and motivate their students. Consider some of the changes in today's educational system and how using the Internet with classes online will help to enrich the learning experience of each child in your class. Your class has a wealth of resources which should be shared. The reports your students write, the poems they create, and the problems they solve, are all valuable and can add to the knowledge-base of this fast-changing world. You can share what is happening in your world by writing a class home page.

One spring, a fourth grade teacher decided to write a Web page with her class. The students were delighted at the idea and the fact they were being included in the planning.

As a group, they discussed the reason for writing the page and what they wanted it to say. The main purpose of the page was to report on the activities which the class experienced during the year, and the secondary purpose was to introduce the teacher to the third-grade students who would be entering this fourth-grade class the next school year. They brainstormed the many activities, field trips, projects, and literature studies completed during the year. Each student was responsible for specific events. The students wrote short descriptive reports on the class actions and created hand-drawn graphics if no photographs were available. The final result of all this writing and review led to a comprehensive review of the year and a marvelous summary of the fourth grade in this classroom. Of course, one of the unexpected results of the site was supplying the parents of the students, both current and future, with a look into the typical workings of this fourth-grade classroom!

This is a section of the Chan/Smith class page.

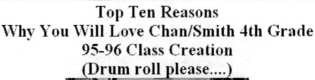

Top Ten Reasons
Why You Will Love Chan/Smith 4th Grade
95-96 Class Creation
(Drum roll please....)

● 10. Science experiments you can eat!
● 9. Math activities you can eat!
● 8. Other projects you can eat!
● 7. You learn with projects, not just reading out of books.

Another reason for classroom teachers to post a home page is to share successful practices with other teachers. When a teacher puts a lot of effort into a project, and is successful, they should share their project with others. There are colleagues all over the world who could benefit from your creative endeavors!

Tony Vincent, a fifth grade teacher in Nebraska, has a classroom full of handheld devices and keyboards, one for each student. The types of things they are going are amazing, and his ideas can be replicated in other classrooms. His Learning in Hand site provides ideas, tips, tricks, and examples of successful use of PDAs to support the instructional process.

Learning in Hand

http://www.teachercreated.com/books/3880

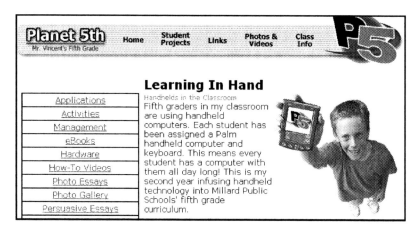

How does having a home page help to infuse new resources into the required curriculum?

Current curriculum is changing. One of the driving forces behind this change is the research and results about new techniques of interdisciplinary learning. Students study in integrated units and can see how all the pieces fit together in learning. For a teacher to innfuse all the disciplines into a unit of study, he or she needs to access many resources and present the information using many different models. Using the Internet as a center to tour a museum, read a current newspaper, or monitor the space shuttle, adds credibility to your study and excitement for the learner.

As you go through the process of creating a class home page, you will explore many resources and will soon want to incorporate many of these sites into your daily lessons. Opening the window to a world of resources gives students the real information they need to prepare for tomorrow. Once you design your class home page, you can designate areas where the resources are linked and are easily at hand for student exploration.

Teachers need to realize, however, that no area of the Internet is truly safe because of the hypertext nature of linking to other sites. Even if you provide students with sites to visit, their Internet use must be monitored carefully. It is recommended that students who are younger than grade seven do not openly search on the Internet using search engines.

Teachers can provision materials and add annotated links to sites on a certain topic to the class home page. If the students are studying the Civil War, a page of resource links and directions for researching, questions about certain pages to evaluate critical reading, and assignments to be completed can also be a part of the page. Students progress though the assignments at their own pace and use the required activities as both formative and summative assessments. This format of a class page incorporates the resources from the Web and makes the student accountable for time spent on the Internet.

Snapshot from a Classroom

A second grade class had been studying Claude Monet and writing poems about his paintings when their technology specialist began visiting with the teacher about writing a class home page. As they talked, she learned the students were in the process of writing a biography of the artist. In no time, the classroom teacher had all the poems typed and saved as text. The technology specialist found some Monet pictures to add to the project, and the page came together.

As an addition, she also listed some resource pages for the students to visit and a form on which students could type answers to some open-ended questions. One of the resources was a tour of Monet's gardens in France, and when they visited the page, the students loved seeing the lily pond which inspired some of Monet's famous paintings. As the classroom teacher saw the students' enthusiasm, she began to plan a weather unit and teamed with another class in the Northeast to compare temperatures. Weather information was the next area of focus on her page.

Poetry Inspired by Paintings of Claude Monet

Written by the Second Graders in Ms. Higgin's Class

Biography of the Artist

Links to other Monet Resources:

⌐Monet Home and Gardens
http://www.monash.edu.au/visarts/diva/monet.html
⌐ Water Lily paintings
http://sunsite.unc.edu/wm/paint/auth/monet/waterlilies/
⌐Louvre - Monet Paintings
http://emf.net/louvre/paint/auth/monet/
⌐Orsay Museum
http://www.paris.org/Musees/Orsay/Collections/Paintings/

Someday teachers will post all of their teaching units on the Web, both for their own use and to share with their classes and classes around the world. Just think of the benefits of having a list available of the literature books you cover each year and reports on those books from last year available for other students to read as exemplars. You can keep all the links you use this year and, when you are ready, update the list of links and add current finds. Teachers are beginning to experiment to see how they can build their units and expand their horizons with these technologies. Many college classes are posted on the Web, and instructors use this tool to post assignments and required reading and to communicate extensive information about their classes. As other teachers see the impact of the online syllabus and timelines for assignments, they will begin to incorporate the process of posting more information for their students.

The following screen captures are from Jon Storslee's pages of information at Arizona State University. Here the students, and anyone else who wants to learn, have access to a wealth of information and resources. He has been using the Web to enhance teacher training for several years and has been an invaluable resource for many educators.

EMC 598 Internet for Teachers

http://www.teachercreated.com/books/3880

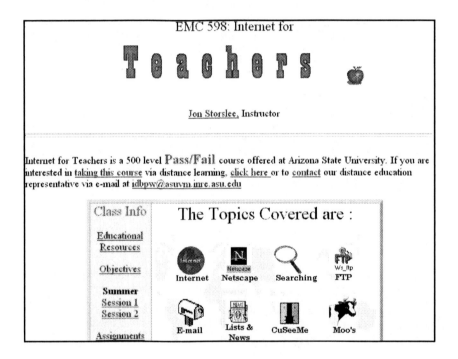

2 Questions to Answer Before Beginning

Class pages can reflect students' creativity and have a significant, powerful impact on student learning. Even if your school or district does not have a home page, consider building a page with your class to share their work and projects.

Here are the results of one teacher's efforts to learn more about using HTML and showing off her students' accomplishments. She plans to share her students' kindergarten experiences with families, grandparents, aunts, and uncles.

On this page, Miss Murphy shares the activities of the students. She also has added links to some favorite sites for students to easily access. This kindergarten teacher is excited about her students using technology in their classroom. She is eager for them to access information and enjoy the experience. She tells about students going to the 4-H farm at the University of Arizona and then, on their own, creating a game in which one student selects the animal sound and the other has to have his or her back to the computer and then guess which animal is making a sound. Kids are very creative when given the proper tools with which to work. You might notice that the 4-H link is one she has written into her class home page.

2 Questions to Answer Before Beginning

The day the page was posted, Miss Murphy's students sent this note to the teacher who put their site online. Can you "hear" the excitement in the class?

> From: pmurphy@mail.tempe3.k12.az.us (PatriciaAnn Murphy)
>
> Organization: Tempe School District No. 3
>
> Subject: Re: Visited your page! WOW
>
> To: shixson@mail.tempe3.k12.az.us
>
> Mrs. Hixson: We got your message. Thank you for putting our page on the Web. We like seeing our class on the computer. Thank you again. Have a happy holiday.
>
> Miss Murphy's Kindergarten Class

The next day this e–mail arrived to the posting teacher, and it was evident that Miss Murphy was hooked on using the Web to share class activities and publish student work.

> From: PatriciaAnn Murphy
>
> Subject: Web Site
>
> To: Susan Hixson
>
> Susan:
>
> Just wanted you to know that the Web site has already met my goals. An uncle of one of my students, who lives in Colorado, wrote that he is going to take this example of a home page to his child's school to show the "power of the Internet." That's quite a compliment! My class is putting stickers on a map of the U.S. to show where we have received e–mail from. We are having fun with it! Thanks again for all of your help.
>
> Pa

2 Questions to Answer Before Beginning

Including student work in the fiber of your class home page significantly enhances the students' realization of the purpose for the projects and motivates student achievement as they are creating for an authentic audience. As you look through many class pages on the Net, you will find examples of teachers who are showing off their students' work and reinforcing their classroom learning.

Hillside Elementary School, Minnesota

http://www.teachercreated.com/books/3880

Mrs. Collin's sixth grade students at Hillside Elementary in Minnesota read many literature books throughout the year. As they write book reports, the reports are posted to help other students understand the books. Here you see a list of the books and a sample of one of the reports.

Hillside's Book Reviews

For more information on this project:

- Lesson Information
- Technical Information: Eight Minute HTML for format information

- The BFG
- Meet Molly
- Blitz #5: End Zone Express
- Amazing Animal Disguises
- In the Dinosaur's Paw
- Eating Ice Cream With a Warewolf
- I Am Fifteen - And I don't Want to Die
- Sideways Stories From Wayside School
- Making the Team
- The Beach House
- Farthest Away Mountain
- Pawn of Prophecy
- My Side of the Mountain
- The War With Grandpa
- The Indian in the Cupboard
- The Boy Who Loved Chocolate
- Piano Lessons Can Be Murder
- Little Big League

Sideways Stories From Wayside School is a very interesting book. Louis Sachar, the author wrote a chapter that told about each character in the story. One of my favorite events in the story was when Mrs. Gorf, a mean teacher turned more than half her class in to apples. Than a couple smart ones turned her in to an apple.

This book is trying to say that everyone and everything is different in a way. It also says things can be the same.

This book starts in an interesting way. The book contains a lot of action but, not a lot of suspense. The main characters change to a different person each chapter so sometimes they show courage and sometimes they don't. I think that this book ends in a very interesting way.

Sideways Stories From Wayside School has black and white pictures at the beginning of each chapter. I think that this book is for grades 3-6. This book has 124 pages in it.

Younger students might have to rely on the teacher to summarize their work. Look at the way that Mrs. Thorpe, a second grade teacher at Archwood School in Canada, includes student work and projects on her pages. She has an extensive class page and shares many class activities.

Mrs. Thorpe's 2nd Grade Page, Archwood School

http://www.teachercreated.com/books/3880

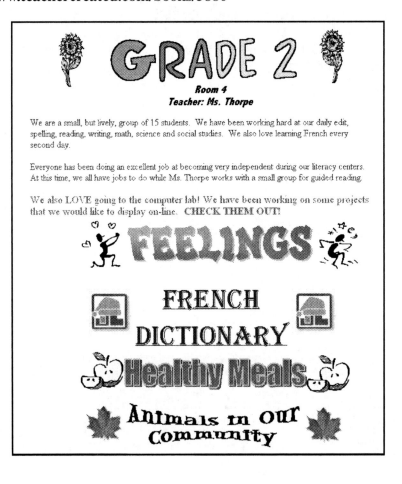

2   Questions to Answer Before Beginning

Other classes are posting poetry, student reports, surveys, science experiments, book reports, and much more. One kindergarten class created a *Kid Pix* project about their future plans with the help of their fifth grade buddies. Here is an example:

Tammy Payton, from Loogootee Elementary West in Indiana posts examples of their schools' projects on the Web. See
http://www.teachercreated.com/books/3880 for the URL.

The potential power of class home pages lies in the hands of the educators who begin to see the wide-range of possibilities and work to take advantage of each one. As you move to the nuts and bolts of how to plan and write a home page, keep in mind some of the examples you have seen and continue to seek out others. Surf to many school pages (find them on Web66) and take a peek at examples of what other teachers are doing. How you present material and how student work can be displayed may be controlled by policies in your district, but you are the key to getting the ideas of students out to the world. Don't hesitate too long. There is so much to be learned, and the risk-takers are out in front, leading the movement in the use of technology and changing the way we teach. Join in all the fun and show off your students' work and your successes to the rest of the world.

2 Questions to Answer Before Beginning

One thing to keep in mind if you post student research projects is to have students include, with their projects, a bibliography of both the print and Internet sources that they consulted. This can help other educators and students who are studying the same topic and want to research it further. Susan Aroldi, a New Jersey library media specialist, has created bibliographic formats for each of the grades, K–6. An edited version is included in the appendices of this book.

2 Questions to Answer Before Beginning

The Challenges of Web Page Philosophy

Each district, school, or class will want to handle the administration and look of the district home pages in a different way. Your district should evaluate the pros and cons of site-based decisions about content and design versus requiring all district home pages to be uniform in content and design. Here are some things to consider as you weigh the benefits and drawbacks of site-based decisions.

Mary Alice Anderson, a media specialist in Winoma, Minnesota, wrote an article for *Technology Connection* entitled "Developing Web Page Policies or Guidelines" which deals with some of the details of creating a school and or classroom Web page.

Schools or districts that have a Web server may consider adopting a policy or guidelines about the development of Web pages and storing them on the school or district's server. Schools that do not have their own Web server but place their pages on a server belonging to an Internet service provider (ISP) may want to develop a policy or guidelines in addition to the policy the ISP may have. Policies or guidelines will help provide some degree of consistency and quality, and provide some general direction as to how the school will be represented to the local Internet community and beyond. These Web guidelines can provide more specifics than are typically found in the more general Internet Acceptable Use Policies schools have adopted. In addition, Web policies or guidelines will help prevent situations which might cause embarrassment or even a lawsuit for the school or district. Specifics will vary with local needs, but basically they should address Web page content, overall responsibility, potential contributors, quality, technical standards, student protection, server access, and a statement of ownership and responsibility. Overall, the content of these guidelines should be clear with the technical information presented in an understandable way.

2 Questions to Answer Before Beginning

Content and Subject Matter

A school's Web presence represents the school to a potentially greater audience than any other medium. The collection of electronic documents can be an excellent way to provide unique information about the school or a means for students and staff to present information about themselves. The Web site must represent the school accurately and fairly. Content policy may address topics such as these:

- Who is our audience—only the school and the local community or also the larger Internet and world community?

- Will there be a central district home page, or will each school or even each department in the school be allowed to create its own "front door"?

- How comprehensive should the site be? For example, will its purpose be to house and publicize all school policies and public information that is normally shared in print, or will it be more limited in scope?

- Should the content pertain only to the school and its curriculum and activities, or may other content be added? For example, will students and staff be permitted to create personal pages about interests and activities that are not school-related?

- How long will student work be kept on the Web site?

- Will there be guidelines specifying how often school information should be updated?

Contributors

- Will Web page/site contributors be limited to the school's student and staff population?

- Will there be a priority for who can have a Web page, or will it be first come, first served, or will all teachers be required to create a Web page?

- Will nonprofit outside groups be allowed to have a presence on the school's server or be directly linked to the school's home page? If so, will they be limited to education-related groups only?

2   Questions to Answer Before Beginning

- Will commercial content and advertising be allowed? For example, some schools may make money from advertising by local businesses; in other situations this could be a conflict of interest with a local ISP.

- Will the district sell server space to outside groups or provide it free of charge? Is this even allowed under their ISP contract?

Quality of Content

Some quality control will provide a way of making sure the school or district is well represented. Specifics to be addressed may include the following:

- Set standards for grammar, spelling, and general overall physical appearance.

- Give suggestions for the quality of student work that will be included.

- Do all students have a right to have their work published on the Web, or will the school select only the best work?

- Set standards for ensuring that content is worthwhile and useful to others.

Technical and Design Standards

Web page design manuals stress the importance of good design principles, designing a page that will work with multiple browsers, and limiting the graphics and glitz. Generally, the recommendation is to design the page with the capability of being viewed over dial-in-access and a 56k modem.

Technical standards may include recommendations regarding the following:

- Overall size or length of a page

- Fonts, graphic size, and format

- Backgrounds, colors, tables, image maps, sound, animations, and special effects

- Any preferred consistency such as an identifying name, logo, or links that should always be present

- Directory structure
- Information about the page's creator and date it was added to the server
- Mail-to links
- Compliance with networking standards, consideration for the conventions of worldwide electronic publishing, and adherence to state and federal laws such as copyright and trademarks

Student and Staff Safeguards

Some information kept by the school is protected under data privacy laws; other information is public. Keep in mind the following considerations:

- What safeguards will there be to prevent questionable material or links to questionable material in the page's immediate links?
- Will staff phone numbers and e–mail addresses be included?
- Will student names be used? (Internet-use guidelines frequently address the importance of not using the names of students in Web documents and in e–mail.)
- Will an e–mail and/or snail address be published?
- Will parental permission to publish a page be required?
- If an individual wishes to publish a page that does not meet the guidelines or policies, will there be due process opportunities for appeal?

Copyright, Ownership, Disclaimers

- Once information is put on the Web, anyone can readily access and copy it. Will you give blanket permission for people to use it, or do you want to encourage people to request permission?
- What responsibility does the school have for inappropriate links that are not immediate links from the school's pages?

2 Questions to Answer Before Beginning

- Will certain information be copyright protected?

- Does the school district accept responsibility for everything that is published?

- What is the relationship to other district policies such as data privacy, copyright, access, and intellectual freedom?

- Is the district or the individual who created a page responsible for the content on the page?

- Is there a form to be signed that allows students to retain the copyright to any work they produce?

Relationship to Other Policies

- Is permission to use information about a student or a picture of a student on the Internet part of the school's general information release policy, or should special permission be included in the Web policy?

- Is the policy free of any contradictions of other district policies such as intellectual freedom, data privacy, copyright, staff ethics, and student behavior?

Server Access

Once a page is prepared it must be put on a Web server. The policy should address who will have that right and responsibility. It may make the most sense for one or two people to have responsibility for the entire Web site, or it may work best to subdivide the site with different individuals having access and responsibilities for different portions of the site. This decision should be based on the size of the site and the skill levels of those responsible. In some districts, a stipend is offered for this job.

Overall Responsibility

This part of the document will address who has overall responsibility for making sure the guidelines or policies are followed. In some districts, responsibility for managing the server and approving page content is primarily given to the library media specialists and the district network specialist. Principals may also be involved in approving information from their buildings.

Finally, the document should have a provision for appropriate intervals for updates and review. As the Web site grows and Webmasters and Web site contributors become more experienced, different needs and considerations will arise. Technical standards are especially likely to change as technology progresses. (Anderson, 1997)

General policies for district Web pages may be formally in place in your district, or they may just be implied. All areas of information should be posted and the legality of such posting needs to be discussed. Discussed is the key word, as all interested parties, such as administrators and teachers, should be represented. Remember that these Web pages will represent an institution of learning and reflect on all members of that educational community. Policies must be approved by the school board and acceptable to members of the school community.

Snapshot from a Classroom

One school has posted pictures of Motorola volunteers working with students and of field trips which were sponsored by the company. They have not included a Motorola insignia, but they do plan to add a link to Motorola Web page and their education department. Is this appropriate? You will need to think about many issues like this as you develop Web policies. This school came online ahead of the rest of the district, so they have functioned without specific rules and regulations. Maybe that will work fine for your district as well, but it is appropriate to discuss these topics before they become issues.

2 Questions to Answer Before Beginning

Quality of student work should be high.

All student work should be well-edited before being posted. After all, this work is a reflection on the school as well as the student and teacher. As educators, there is a responsibility to display work which students will be proud of sharing. Spelling and grammatical errors should be corrected, and all citations included should be in an acceptable format. These formats are outlined at the end of this book.

Should parental permission be obtained before writing and projects can be posted?

Some districts require permission slips to be signed for all work each time it is posted. At one district, not only photographs of students but also artwork and writing must be sent home with a note to ask permission for the work to be included on the class home page. This is done to inform the student and parent that the student still retains the copyright of the work. Unfortunately, these extra steps may discourage some teachers from including student work on their pages. It is hoped that as the process is refined, a general letter of permission to publish could be signed so that student work could be more readily available to a wider audience. It is suggested that only student initials be used when posting work. At the present time many districts have a generic letter of permission which parents sign to allow students to have their pictures taken by the press which does not usually include permission to post students' pictures on the Web. As a safety measure, students' pictures should never be posted on the Web.

Whitewater School District in Whitewater, Wisconsin, has posted their parental permission policy on the Internet and has granted permission on the site for all to copy and utilize it. The following page contains a version of the document that has been reduced in size.

Parent Permission Form for World Wide Web Publishing of Student Work

Name of Student _____

School _____

Name of Parent _____

We understand that our daughter or son's artwork or writing is under consideration for publication on the World Wide Web, a part of the Internet. We further understand that the work will appear with a copyright notice prohibiting the copying of such work without express written permission.

In the event anyone requests such permission, those requests will be forwarded to us. No home address or telephone number will appear with such work.

We grant permission for the World Wide Web publishing as described above until June 20__. A copy of all such publishing will be printed out and brought home for us to see.

Name _____ Date _____

Name _____ Date _____

I, the student, also give my permission for such publishing.

Name _____ Date _____

Permission is granted to copy and use this form.
(Whitewater School District, 1997)

Can student names be attached to their work?

Some districts allow only first names, while others want no student names posted. It is a good policy never to list names or initials of students with pictures (if you decide to use pictures) and only to use initials when identifying information is placed on student work. Some districts do not have a policy in place and encourage teachers to be careful, usually recommending that less is better. This is a topic you will need to address with your school.

Districts sometimes set strict standards for the school Web pages and dictate the format as well how the graphics will be used. If your district is just beginning to establish guidelines about Web page style, you might want to be involved. There are some districts which require that all schools in the district use the same format for their school pages in order to keep the look and feel of the site consistent.

Jamie McKenzie, in his book, *Net Profit in a Post Modem World*, writes an informative chapter entitled "Home Sweet Home: Creating WWW Pages Which Deliver." Following are the main points of the chapter. The book and associated Web page cover these aspects of Web page design in much greater detail.

Home Sweet Home

http://www.teachercreated.com/books/3880

A good WWW site performs at least three functions:

1. The site points internal users to outside information resources which are curriculum related and developmentally appropriate, providing clear indexing and adequate description of these resources so that staff and students can make wise choices and move rapidly through Cyberspace toward the information they need.

2. The site points external visitors and internal users to valuable internal curriculum resources such as artifacts and data regarding local history, local water quality, or student-generated productions and performances of various kinds.

3. The site introduces external visitors to the school.

These functions lead logically to a number of design principles which may guide the building of pages. They are listed and explained here to support the thinking, planning, and invention of those who are launching a site on the World Wide Web.

The Tenets of Effective Web Site Design

Tenet Number One: Less is more. Take a minimalist approach to page design. Employ graphics only when the visual content contributes meaning to the page.

Tenet Number Two: Distinguish between menu pages (those that help the visitors move through the site) and data pages.

Tenet Number Three: Maintain smoothly gliding formats by repeating basic formats.

Tenet Number Four: Provide visitors with enough information to make wise choices.

Tenet Number Five: Create menus which are logically comprehensive and coherent, employing headings which are meaningful.

Tenet Number Six: Provide navigational tools in systematically consistent fashion.

Tenet Number Seven: Maintain consistent formats and avoid a hodgepodge of random designs.

Tenet Number Eight: Include appropriate copyright notices on every page.

Tenet Number Nine: Include snail and e–mail addresses as well as contact names and institutional affiliations on major menu pages.

Tenet Number Ten: Consider at least one year of site development before proceeding with the first page.

Tenet Number Eleven: Employ thoughtful file-naming conventions to minimize the need for subdirectories and folders.

Tenet Number Twelve: Balance breadth and depth when considering the structure of menus and files. If a page offers more than a hundred menu items, it is too broad and should be condensed into categories.

Tenet Number Thirteen: When linking to other WWW locations, strip away time-wasting top levels of those sites, provide addresses which take users directly to good information, and include thorough annotations explaining what can be found at those locations.

Tenet Number Fourteen: Beware of casual endorsements.

Tenet Number Fifteen: Include disclaimers whenever individuals may be expressing personal opinions which are not shared by the school or the school district.

Tenet Number Sixteen: Do not post identifying information and photographs of individual children.

Tenet Number Seventeen: Have a staff committee review all materials before publishing on the WWW.

Tenet Number Eighteen: Avoid providing home pages for individuals.

(McKenzie, 1996)

William Penn School District (PA)

http://www.teachercreated.com/books/3880

These screen captures illustrate how these Web pages from schools in the William Penn School District are consistent despite including unique information on each page. These schools have no personalized graphics, but the individuality of the pages is expressed in the content. The background colors, layout, and graphics are the same, and each school must submit specific written information about their school. Information is then posted and connected to the district page. By being efficient, the entire district has been able to get school pages posted for their schools.

2 Questions to Answer Before Beginning

Snapshot from a Classroom

A technology specialist works with many schools which have just come online over the past year. Each school is working to get a school page posted soon, and it is very interesting to see how they go about the process. He usually writes the HTML for the pages, but he encourages each staff to be thoroughly involved in the design and approval of the product. At some schools, the principal will take the lead and just tell the technology specialist to use certain information and create a page. After a mock page is ready, it is taken to the staff or a technology committee for changes and suggestions. There are always changes, and that is the way it should be, as the school claims ownership for the page. Members of the staff must feel the page represents their school, and therefore they will be more motivated to complete their section and display their class activities with pride.

Other school home pages are designed by the technology committee at the school, and then pages of information and disks of text are given to this technology specialist to string together. Again, changes are the norm, but he does appreciate the initial input from the staff. He usually asks to meet with the committee and find this a valuable time to discuss the objectives of the page and how it will represent the school. After all, visitors to the school page should get a feeling of school pride and be introduced to the school's academic focus.

One of his schools has a lab assistant who wanted to do all the work, and this assistant has spent many hours learning HTML, scanning pictures, and testing the pages. This page is now up and ready for others to see, but during the process, only the lab assistant learned how Web pages are created. Because he kept such tight control of the project, it is doubtful that many other teachers at the school will feel free to begin to post their information. If the pages become a joint project, teachers learn more about what is needed and assist in the design and development, and the information can be compiled and posted faster.

2 Questions to Answer Before Beginning

Each of the school pages has a different feel and uses different graphics, colors, and even backgrounds. The schools in this district have taken to heart that they are different, and their home pages proclaim their individuality. All pages are works in progress and will never be complete. One of the strengths of the Web is that it is dynamic and encourages constant change and revision.

How much do you want to tell the public about your district or school, and how should it be presented?

If an open-door policy is a part of your school and community culture, then the sky is the limit as to how much the school or district should post and needs to post on its pages.

Posting Ideas for Districts:

- School calendars, especially if there are many varied calendars among the schools in the district

- Lunch menus for the month

- School board minutes and agendas (They might be informative to some and are a part of the public record.)

- Numbers of students and teachers in buildings

- Average class sizes and policies on class size

- Links to state department of education information

- Performances and standardized test scores

- Information about special programs for reading, math, science, gifted, special education, etc.

- Maps of the district with locations of the schools and neighborhoods which attend them

- Bus routes along with times and addresses of pick-ups

- Beginning and dismissal times

- Phone numbers and e-mail addresses of key people in the district or school to call for questions

- Anything that your district or school believes would be of interest to a family who lives in or is moving to your district

Posting Ideas for Schools:

- School address, phone number, contact people, and a map of location (These maps can be easily linked to MapBlast, an online mapping tool available at **www.mapblast.com**.)

- Attendance area map with bus stops marked

- Calendar for the year, with holidays, assemblies, parties, book fairs, evening events, conference days, PTA meetings, and other special events

- A list of staff and their phone extensions and e–mail addresses

- Mission statement and school beliefs

- Links to classroom pages

- Messages from the principal

- Calls for volunteers with directions on how to sign up and information about any requirements and training

- Information about school fund-raisers and other ongoing projects

- School's state evaluation report

- Links to special projects conducted by the students and teachers

Nathaniel H. Wixon Middle School, South Dennis, MA

http://www.teachercreated.com/books/3880

Here is an example of a school page which effectively includes some of the items listed on the preceding page. Nathaniel H. Wixon Middle School in South Dennis, MA uses a pleasing format to make accessing information easy for the reader.

Who can post changes and new Web home pages?

If your district has its own Web server and is hosting home pages, or is hosting the pages on a server owned by someone else, decisions need to be made as to who will have the permission to send changes and corrections to the Web site.

It is prudent to limit the number of accounts on the server and have strict rules about what will be displayed under the district's name. You may want to allow teachers to qualify by attending some training and then getting an account on the server. This would allow the educators to post information as often as they please. They would be able to make changes to their own pages, update information, post homework, display current student work, post student newsletters, and so on.

There should be limitations on the type of information offered on the Web, but the timely access to the server for updating information is crucial and can most effectively be used by the trained user.

As more teachers want to publish Internet information, at least one person at each school will need to have access to the district server for posting these files. If you are trying to encourage the use of an evolving technology, allow for each participant to explore its capabilities. Of course, there might be forms to be signed for legal permission and some limits on content, but most teachers should not mind adhering to the guidelines. Hopefully, these regulations will focus on safety and not affect the creativity of the projects as they evolve.

Teachers will see the benefits of posting and updating information and make it a priority in their projects. Imagine the impact when parents see homework assignments, spelling lists, and outstanding student work on a regular basis. Parents accessing the class page will find valuable information and become more active participants in their students' learning.

School Page Planning

Once you have set objectives for your page and are aware of district requirements, it is time to formulate the plan. To ensure total school involvement, it is very important that as many staff members as possible be included and all their ideas seriously considered. The more the team works together, the more creative ideas will be generated. When the staff feels ownership of the page, they will begin to develop it into a true work of art. Keep in mind not everything has to be included on the front/home page, and so it is suggested that you begin with a chart which allows you to set priorities and organize your thoughts. Using a storyboard or concept-mapping software can be a very effective method of planning.

Part 3: Planning Pages

School Page Planning

Plan the Content and Layout of Your Web Structure Page

The more planning you do at the beginning of the process, the easier the process will proceed. By building a Web layout, you will begin to see more clearly where the links on the home page will lead and also what information needs to be collected to create the page. It does not matter if this is a school page or one for your class since the organization is very similar; the topics are just altered to be more meaningful to the intended audience.

It is suggested you write out your plan or use the template found here to begin the process of organization. Make copies of the template and physically arrange the pages to show your organization. Put a title and HTML address at the top of each page to identify it in your structure. This will help as you begin to create your documents. You can name the pages things like "class projects," and when you have created your Web document, it can be linked to "projects.html" for easy reference.

Naming Web Pages:

- Keep the page names simple, yet descriptive
- Use all lowercase letters
- Names should not be too long.
- Include no spaces in the Web page file name
- Combining letters and numbers is acceptable
- Some ISPs require your files to end in html vs. htm

On the next page you see a planning format to use to fill in the who, what, and how. The template which follows it is a completed version to give you an idea of what might be placed in the blanks.

3 Planning Pages

Planning Front Home Page

_____.html

Title of Page:

Purpose of the Page:

Graphics Included:

Topics Covered	Link Address	Who's in Charge

3 Planning Pages

Planning Front Home Page

Planning Front Home Page

_____bighill__.html

Title of Page: Big Hill School

Purpose of the Page:	communicate with community/ show student work/ introduce staff/show school

Graphics Included:
school picture, dots, lines, mailbox

Topics Covered	Link Address	Who's in Charge
Special Service music/art/read/ resources/etc.	special.html	Mrs. Brown
Class Page	classes.html	Mr. Hunt
School Calendar	calendar.html	Ms. Smith
Curriculum Resources	resources.html	Mr. Jones

3 Planning Pages

For each of the pages which are linked off the front page you will want to use a separate template to note

- the graphics to be used

- the file name of the intended Web page

- links to other resources and notes for placement of links which return you to the front page.

- the person responsible for maintaining the page

All of the completed pages can be laid out to show how they are linked and tied to the front home page. Creating the pages and getting all the links organized is a very structured task.

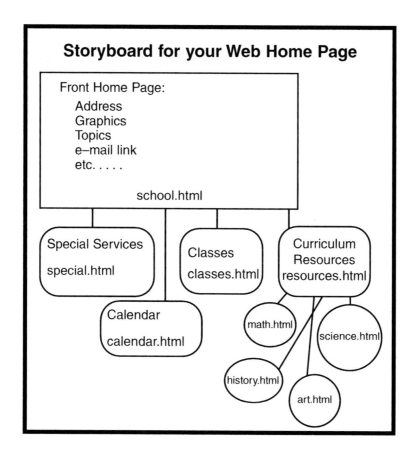

3 Planning Pages

Design Your School Page

Once you have the links named and know the main topics you want to display, it is time to design your front page and all subsequent pages. The best way to get ideas of what works best and is most pleasing to the eye is to surf the Net for school pages which others have created. Take a look at some of the sites listed in Technology and Learning's "School Web Site of the Month Archive" (**http://www.teachercreated.com/books/3880**) As you look at each school site, remember that only a portion of the page will show as it loads in your browser. For a positive first impression while the visitors to your school's Web page is waiting for all the information to load, be sure that something of interest is placed at the top of the page. Study all other school pages with a critical eye. Many school pages are well-designed, but they are all different and also quickly create a unique feeling about their school.

Carefully note how these exemplary school pages have incorporated the following:

- photographs
- original graphics
- lines/dots/icons (colors and sizes)
- organization of the text and lists
- e–mail return addresses
- amount of information presented on the page/organization
- topics covered
- the time it took to load the page

Don't be satisfied with this limited selection of school pages; search Web66 to find thousands of examples. Remember that you are looking for the best design to present information about your school.

3   Planning Pages

Web66

http://www.teachercreated.com/books/3880

As you examine these pages, take note of the design format each school has used to present information about the school. Each page uses photographs and graphics in different ways to paint a picture of the school and portray a feeling about the school. As you examine the sample pages, think about the school they represent and whether the pages make you want to know more about this school. If you take a look at elementary, middle, and high school sites, you will quickly realize the age of students doesn't necessarily determine the design of the page.

Please note that all school Web pages nearly always include an e–mail link to receive communications from visitors, and this link is usually located at the bottom of the page so it can be used after seeing the entire page. Text and pictures are arranged to systematically lead the visitor down the page to find the link they seek.

You will want to take the best ideas of each presentation you view on the Web and begin to incorporate them into your own school page design. Take notes about the pages you find most pleasing or print out a copy of the page for later reference or to share with your committee.

To print a copy of a home page you are viewing on your Web browser is an easy process. Just press the print button on your Web browser toolbar. (Or choose "Print" from the File menu.) Do be aware of the fact that you will print the entire page, and it may be quite long. You are printing an entire electronic page and not just the page you see on your screen at one time. Unless you have one of the newer browsers, you will not have the option to print the background and background colors.

3 Planning Pages

To figure out how to make your page use some of the same effects as those you are viewing, you need to save the source code which is the HTML coding of the page. (Some of the newer Web pages are created with software that will not show you the raw code and some of the pages are created on the fly.) Applications for this saved source code will be discussed later. As you conduct your research, it is the perfect time to begin to save some of the pages of code. As you write your page, you will find this collection of coding valuable. You are encouraged to create a folder on your hard drive and begin to save captured pages, pages of source code, and collected graphics from freeware collections.

- On a Macintosh, to capture the source codes of the page using *Netscape*, pull down "Edit—Show Document Source." A new screen will open which displays all of the coding which was used to write the page you are viewing. This code can then be saved on your computer. After saving, just close the window, and you will be back at the original page.

- On an Windows machine, the process is a bit different. You can view the source code by choosing "View—Document Source" from the *Netscape* menu bar. However, you cannot print from this screen. In order to save the source code, just choose "File—Save As" from the original browser window and make sure the file type you are saving is an HTML document. Although it has an .html extension, it is still just a simple text document and may be opened in any text editor or word processor.

- In *Internet Explorer*, the menu choice of "View—Source" will provide you with the source code and you can save print it right out of the browser on the source code page.

While you are on the Internet and see graphics which might enhance your page, you can capture them and save copies in your Web page folder. Make sure that permission to use the graphics you are capturing is given on the Web page. If nothing is noted, you will need to obtain permission to use them. There are many libraries of free-use graphics on the Internet. (See page 133.)

It is very important to respect copyrights and the premise of intellectual property. Brad Templeton has written the following revealing, helpful essay.

10 Big Myths About Copyright Explained

Note that this is an essay about copyright myths. It assumes you know at least what copyright is — basically, the legal exclusive right of the author of a creative work to control the copying of that work. (If you didn't know that, check out Hall Davidson's site which is includes this chart with everything educators need to know about copyright at **http://www.teachercreated.com/books/3880**)

1. "If it doesn't have a copyright notice, it's not copyrighted." This was true in the past, but today almost all major nations follow the Berne copyright convention. For example, in the USA almost everything created privately and originally after April 1, 1989, is copyrighted and protected whether it has a notice or not. The attitude you should assume for other people's works is that they are copyrighted and may not be copied unless you know otherwise. There are some old works that lost protection without notice, but frankly you should not risk it unless you know for sure.

   It is true that a notice strengthens the protection by warning people and by allowing one to get more and different damages, but it is not necessary. If it looks copyrighted, you should assume it is. This applies to pictures, too. You may not scan pictures from magazines and post them to the Net, and if you come upon something unknown, you shouldn't post that either.

   The correct form for a notice is

   "Copyright [dates] by [author/owner]"

   You can use C in a circle © or (C) instead of "Copyright," but "©" has never been given legal force. The phrase "All Rights Reserved" used to be required in some nations but is now not needed.

2. "If I don't charge for it, it's not a violation." False. Whether you charge can affect the damages awarded in court, but that's essentially the only difference. It's still a violation if you give it away—and there can still be heavy damages if you hurt the commercial value of the property.

3. "If it's posted to Usenet, it's in the public domain." False. Nothing modern is in the public domain anymore unless the owner explicitly puts it in the public domain*. Explicitly means you have a note from the author/owner saying, "I grant this to the public domain." Those exact words or words very much like them are required.

Some argue that posting to Usenet implicitly grants permission to everybody to copy the posting within fairly wide bounds, and others feel that Usenet is an automatic store-and-forward network where all the thousands of copies made are done at the command (rather than the consent) of the poster. This is a matter of some debate, but even if the former is true (and in this writer's opinion we should all pray it isn't true), it simply would suggest posters are implicitly granting permissions "for the sort of copying one might expect when one posts to Usenet," and in no case is this a placement of material into the public domain. It is important to remember that when it comes to the law, computers never make copies; only human beings make copies. Computers are given commands, not permission. Only people can be given permission. Furthermore, it is very difficult for an implicit license to supersede an explicitly stated license that the copier was aware of.

* Copyrights can expire after a long time, putting something into the public domain, and there are some fine points on this issue regarding older copyright law versions. However, none of this applies to an original article posted to Usenet.

Note that all this assumes the poster had the right to post the item in the first place. If the poster didn't, then all the copies are pirated, and no implied license or theoretical reduction of the copyright can take place.

Note that granting something to the public domain (PD) is a complete abandonment of all rights. You can't make something "PD for noncommercial use." If your work is PD, other people can even modify just one byte and put their names on it.

4. "My posting was just fair use!" See other notes on fair use for a detailed answer, but bear the following in mind:

The "fair use" exemption to copyright law was created to allow things such as commentary, parody, news reporting, research, and education about copyrighted works without the permission of the author. Intent and damage to the commercial value of the work are important considerations. Are you reproducing an article from the New York Times because you needed to in order to criticize the quality of the New York Times or because you couldn't find time to write your own story or didn't want your readers to have to pay for the New York Times Web site?

The first is probably fair use; the others probably aren't.

Fair use is almost always a short excerpt and almost always attributed. (One should not use more of the work than is necessary to make the commentary.) It should not harm the commercial value of the work in the sense of people no longer needing to buy it (which is another reason why reproduction of the entire work is generally forbidden).

Note that most inclusion of text in Usenet follow-ups is for commentary and reply, and it doesn't damage the commercial value of the original posting (if it has any), and as such it is fair use. Fair use isn't an exact doctrine, either. The court decides if the right to comment overrides the copyright on an individual basis in each case. There have been cases that go beyond the bounds of what I say above, but in general they don't apply to the typical Net claim of fair use. It's a risky defense to attempt.

Facts and ideas can't be copyrighted, but their expression and structure can. You can always write the facts in your own words.

5. "If you don't defend your copyright you lose it." "Somebody has that name copyrighted!" False.

Copyright is effectively never lost these days unless explicitly given away. You also can't "copyright a name" or anything short like that, such as almost all titles. You may be thinking of trademarks which do apply to names and can be weakened or lost if not defended.

You generally trademark terms by using them to refer to your brand of a generic type of product or service. Like an "Apple" computer. Apple Computer "owns" that word applied to computers, even though it is also an ordinary word. Apple Records owns it when applied to music. Neither owns the word on its own, only in context, and owning a mark doesn't mean complete control—see a more detailed treatise on this law for details.

You can't use somebody else's trademark in a way that would unfairly hurt the value of the mark, or in a way that might make people confuse you with the real owner of the mark, or in a way which might allow you to profit from the mark's good name. For example, if I were giving advice on music videos, I would be very wary of trying to label my works with a name like "mtv."

6. "If I make up my own stories but base them on another work, my new work belongs to me." False. Copyright law is quite explicit that the making of what are called "derivative works" — works based on or derived from another copyrighted work — is the exclusive province of the owner of the original work. This is true even though the making of these new works is a highly creative process. If you write a story using settings or characters from somebody else's work, you need that author's permission.

Yes, that means almost all "fan fiction" is a copyright violation. If you want to write a story about Jim Kirk and Mr. Spock, you need Paramount's permission, plain and simple. Now, as it turns out, many, but not all, holders of popular copyrights turn a blind eye to "fan fiction" or even subtly encourage it because it helps them. Make no mistake, however, that it is entirely up to them whether to do that.

There is one major exception—parody. The fair use provision says that if you want to make fun of something like Star Trek, you don't need their permission to include Mr. Spock. This is not a loophole; you can't just take a nonparody and claim it is one on a technicality. The way "fair use" works is you get sued for copyright infringement, and you admit you did infringe but that your infringement was a fair use. A subjective judgement is then made.

7. "They can't get me; defendants in court have powerful rights!" Copyright law is mostly civil law. If you violate copyright you would usually get sued, not charged with a crime. "Innocent until proven guilty" is a principle of criminal law, as is "proof beyond a reasonable doubt." Sorry, but in copyright suits, these don't apply the same way or at all. It's mostly which side and set of evidence the judge or jury accepts or believes more, though the rules vary based on the type of infringement. In civil cases you can even be made to testify against your own interests.

8. "Oh, so copyright violation isn't a crime or anything?" Actually, recently in the USA, commercial copyright violation involving more than 10 copies and value over $2,500 was made a felony. So watch out. (At least you get the protections of criminal law.) On the other hand, don't think you're going to get people thrown in jail for posting your e-mail. The courts have much better things to do than that. This is a fairly new, untested statute.

9. "It doesn't hurt anybody—in fact it's free advertising." It's up to the owner to decide if they want the free ads or not. If they want them, they will be sure to contact you. Don't rationalize about whether it hurts the owner or not; ask him. Usually that's not too hard to do. At one time Clarinet published the very funny Dave Barry column to a large and appreciative Usenet audience for a fee, but some person didn't ask and forwarded it to a mailing list, got caught, and the newspaper chain that employs Dave Barry pulled the column from the Net, angering everybody who enjoyed it. Even if you can't think of how the author or owner gets hurt, think about the fact that piracy on the Net hurts everybody who wants a chance to use this wonderful new technology to do more than read other people's flame wars.

10. "They e–mailed me a copy, so I can post it." To have a copy is not to have the copyright. All the e–mail you write is copyrighted. However, e–mail is not, unless previously agreed, secret. So you can certainly report on e–mail you are sent and reveal what it says. You can even quote parts of it to demonstrate. Frankly, somebody who sues over an ordinary message would almost surely get no damages because the message has no commercial value, but if you want to stay strictly within the law, you should ask first. On the other hand, don't become upset if somebody posts e–mail you sent them. If it was an ordinary nonsecret personal letter of minimal commercial value with no copyright notice (like 99.9% of all e–mail), you probably won't get any damages if you sue them. Note as well that, the law aside, keeping private correspondence private is a courtesy one should usually honor.

3 Planning Pages

11. "So I can't ever reproduce anything?" Myth #11 (I didn't want to change the now-famous title of this article) is actually one sometimes generated in response to this list of 10 myths. No, copyright isn't an ironclad lock on what can be published. Indeed, many argue that by providing rewards to authors, it encourages them to not just allow but fund the publication and distribution of works so that they reach far more people than they would if they were free or unprotected—and unpromoted. However, it must be remembered that copyright has two main purposes, namely the protection of the author's right to obtain commercial benefit from valuable work and, more recently, the protection of the author's general right to control how a work is used.

While copyright law makes it technically illegal to reproduce almost any new creative work (other than under fair use) without permission, if the work is unregistered and has no real commercial value, it gets very little protection. The author in this case can sue for an injunction against the publication, actual damages from a violation, and possibly court costs. Actual damages means actual money potentially lost by the author due to publication, plus any money gained by the defendant. But if a work has no commercial value, such as a typical e–mail message or conversational Usenet posting, the actual damages will be zero. Only the most vindictive (and rich) author would sue when no damages are possible, and the courts don't look kindly on vindictive plaintiffs unless the defendants are even more vindictive.

The author's right to control what is done with a work, however, has some validity, even if it has no commercial value. If you feel you need to violate a copyright "because you can get away with it because the work has no value," you should ask yourself why you're doing it. In general, respecting the rights of creators to control their creations is a principle many advocate adhering to.

In addition, while more often than not people claim a "fair use" copying incorrectly, fair use is a valid concept necessary to allow the criticism of copyrighted works and their creators through examples. But please read more about it before you do it.

3 Planning Pages

In Summary

- These days, almost all things are copyrighted the moment they are written, and no copyright notice is required.

- Copyright is still violated whether you charged money or not; only damages are affected by that.

- Postings to the Net are not granted to the public domain and don't grant you any permission to do further copying except perhaps the sort of copying the poster might have expected in the ordinary flow of the Net.

- Fair use is a complex doctrine meant to allow certain valuable social purposes. Ask yourself why you are republishing what you are posting and why you couldn't have just rewritten it in your own words.

- Copyright is not lost because you don't defend it; that's a concept from trademark law. The ownership of names is also from trademark law, so don't say somebody has a name copyrighted.

- Fan fiction and other work derived from copyrighted works is a copyright violation.

- Copyright law is mostly civil law where the special rights of criminal defendants you hear so much about don't apply. Watch out, however, as new laws are moving copyright violation into the criminal realm.

- Don't rationalize that you are helping the copyright holder; often it's not that hard to ask permission.

- Posting e–mail is technically a violation, but revealing facts from e–mail you got isn't, and for almost all typical e–mail, nobody could wring any damages from you for posting it.

- The law doesn't do much to protect works with no commercial value. (Templeton, 1996)

3   Planning Pages

Now that you are familiar with the items that are legal to copy, it is now a simple process to capture graphics from a graphics gallery on the Web.

On a Macintosh computer, you only need to place the cursor on the graphic and press and hold down on the mouse button. A screen will appear and ask if you want to save the graphic or make a link. It is best to save the graphic because if you want to insert the graphic into your page, it will load faster if it is located on your site and many graphics sites do not want you to link to a graphic while it is located their server. Once you select "save graphic," you will then select your Web folder and save it there.

On a Windows machine, simply hold down the right mouse button as you are positioned over the graphic, and a menu will pop up which will allow you to "save image as" to a folder of your choice.

With either machine, do not change the extension (gif or jpeg) that appears in the filename. While changing a file's extension does not change the format of the graphic, you will be unable to open the file from the desktop by double-clicking on it.

Following are samples of school home pages and some information about the pages. You can log on and view them on your computer. (Links to all of them are found at **http://www.teachercreated.com/books/3880**) You may find a page which has a design that you really like and want to print out to use as a reference or save. Also note that the load time as you view the pages and decide the pros and cons for your potential audience if you use large graphics on your opening page.

3 Planning Pages

Nauset Public Schools, Orleans, MA

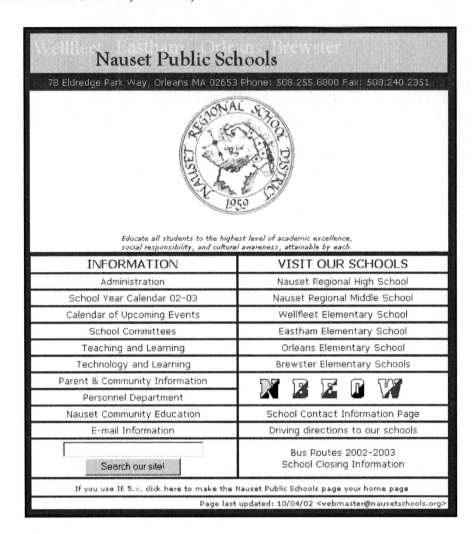

3 Planning Pages

The boxes that appear on Web pages that look like a grid are formed by using HTML coding to create "tables." Notice on this page the use of tables creates nicely arranged boxes in which topics are linked. This is an effective way of presenting information. Graphics are incorporated to pretty up the page, but they are not overwhelming. This district front page presents an engaging image of a learning environment and seems like an active place to spend your days teaching and learning. This page also has a date indicating the last time it was updated and provides useful information for the community. There are many forms of information linked from this page.

Buckman Arts Magnet Elementary School in Portland, Oregon

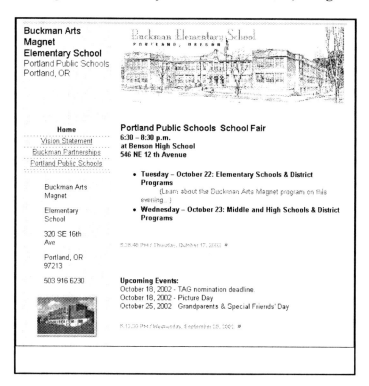

3 Planning Pages

Notice the great line drawing of the school which creates less loading time and the judicious use of white space to divide the information on the page. This page is easy to read and navigate for the user.

George R. Hanaford Elementary School in East Greenwich Rhode Island

This page welcomes you with a pleasing interface and only essential information. It is truly a "home page." This is a different approach to welcoming a visitor. Almost of the page is seen in the browser window and you are not required to scroll down to find more information. The links to the rest of the information are built into the navigation bar on the right; just touch the word and you will go to the appropriate page.

3 Planning Pages

Avon Middle School, Avon CT

A well-done front page leads to a wealth of information including an instructional message from the principal, links to the teachers Web pages, and a scrolling "important notices" area on the front page. This is an easy to use site with useful information for parents and teachers alike.

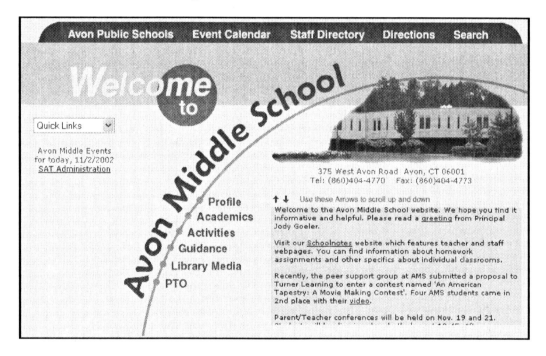

3 Planning Pages

Woodmere Elementary School in Portland, Oregon

This school page has links for students, teachers, and parents. It also has links to resources so that you can begin to search the Net quickly on any educational information. In addition, this site includes samples of student work and projects and a historical photographic essay of the school. These "exhibits" work well in attracting the students and their parents to the site.

HOME STUDENT WORK MORE ABOUT WOODMERE INTERNET RESOURCES WOODMERE HISTORY

WELCOME TO WOODMERE!

Updated on October 8, 2002

Woodmere is a SMART School! To find out more about SMART (Start Making A Reader Today) or to volunteer to be a reader, visit their website or come in to Woodmere and ask about our program.

The Portland Tribune recently featured an article about Woodmere. Read it here!

Teachers can go to InsidePPS for resources.

This is the place to go for school closure information.

Teacher's Online Multimedia Library catalog and order system. Have your employee ID number and password ready.

Woodmere School has been on Duke Street for almost 90 years. Take a look at Woodmere as it used to be.

Please scroll down to get to the search engines.

Woodmere Elementary School
7900 S.E. Duke St.
Portland, OR 97206

Woodmere Elementary School is located in Southeast Portland , Oregon and is part of Portland Public Schools , (English), (Spanish), (Russian), (Vietnamese) , a PK-12 district with an enrollment of approximately 58,000 students, approximately 100 school sites, and 50 special-needs sites throughout the metropolitan area.

3 Planning Pages

Center Street School, Williston, NY

This appealing elementary school page is a joint effort of parents, teachers, and students, all which comes together to provide a look at news, student work, and upcoming events at the school.

3 Planning Pages

Boulder High School in Boulder, Colorado

This site includes all the relevant links in an easy-to-use navigation bar on the left. It contains links to important information about the school, an e–mail contact, and a last-modified date. The design is simple, and you see that page design can be simple and still fill all the needs of a school.

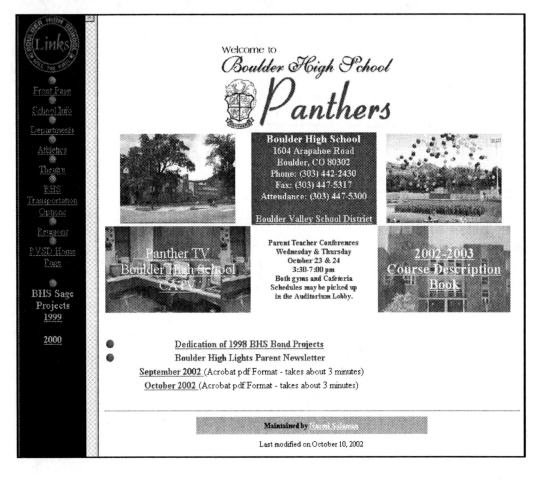

3 Planning Pages

Blue Valley High School in Overland Park, Kansas

This site utilizes some of the newer Web technologies to create a page with class and distinction. There are roll-over menus which give the user a sub-menu when they put their mouse over the menu item. There is a changing picture slide show near the bottom of the page. It is made clear that with a large percentage of students going on to college, this school is serious about academics.

3 Planning Pages

Now you are ready to create your own design.

It is always a balancing act to limit the time it takes the browser to load your page and the creative presentation, which can keep the reader focused long enough to read about your school and follow many of the links. The goal of your school page design is to take the best ideas you have seen and weave them into your school image. This front-home page for your school sets a tone for the reader.

Working with your team, you will begin to find a format that works best to present the image and spirit your school wants to broadcast. Remember that change is fairly easy, and items can always be added or deleted quickly, so the page is never complete. Stay away from "under construction" graphics if possible since you want to present a page that has been thought about and worked on carefully. Don't mount the pages on the Internet for all to see until they are fairly complete. A half-done page with bits and pieces of information is not the image of your school you want to portray.

Use a desktop publishing program, such as *Microsoft Publisher*, to create a mock-up of your front page. No need to gather the graphics at this point, but just put in placeholders that you and the team can easily move around. Do remember, however, that making a Web page look exactly like a desktop-published document is just about impossible. It is probably best to start your mock-up with a two-column table, which is what you will need to do for the Web page.

3 Planning Pages

<table>
<tr><td colspan="2" align="center">

Big Hill School

</td></tr>
<tr><td colspan="2" align="center">School photo here</td></tr>
<tr><td align="center">School
mascot
picture</td><td>Mission statement
_____
_____
_____</td></tr>
<tr><td>Welcome to school
_____
_____
_____</td><td align="center">Principal
picture</td></tr>
<tr><td align="right">More about the school</td><td>School Calendar</td></tr>
<tr><td align="right">Class Pages</td><td>Curriculum Resources</td></tr>
<tr><td align="right">Special Services</td><td>Student Gallery</td></tr>
<tr><td colspan="2" align="center">Big Hill School
4723 S. Big Hill Road
Highup, AZ 85345
602-345-5678
Fax 602-876-5432</td></tr>
<tr><td colspan="2" align="center">Send comments and suggestions to Mrs. Brown (e-mail address)
Date of last update:</td></tr>
</table>

3 Planning Pages

Class Page Planning

Although this section discusses classroom home pages, all of the information and examples shown can easily be transferred to posting class activities or departmental information at the middle school or high school level. As you surf the Internet for examples of class pages, you will find that elementary schools usually have a section specifically for class information. Middle and secondary schools usually display under different the different subject categories. You will have to adjust this to fit your situation and interests.

Plan the Contents and Layout of Your Page

Planning a class page can generate a tremendous excitement in the classroom and be a motivating factor throughout the school year. Whether you decide to create the Web page on your own or with the help of your class of students, the response to the pages can be pretty exciting for everyone. The process you need to follow is the same whether you are going at it alone or with a group. This is the place where the comfort level of the teacher is very important. If you are experienced with including your students in group activities, then tackling the design and creation of a home page for the class may feel natural to you. Be comfortable with your decision and then get started.

Begin with a discussion of the purpose of the page. Stress the fact you are creating an online image of your class and want that image to reflect the true work which is being done each day. Although you think your readers will be parents and other students, you don't know for sure who will see the page. Your class must be prepared to display their best work and creative ideas for whoever winds up being the audience.

3   Planning Pages

After a focus for the page has been established, begin to brainstorm what information you want to include on the home page. Write down the ideas so they can be revisited and revised or begin the process by filling in some ideas on a form or using concept-mapping software such as Inspiration.

Many ideas for topics to include on a classroom home page are listed here, but your students will come up with many more. You will have to decide whether you want to limit topics and how complex a project you are willing to create. The amount of time you have to work on the page may determine the scope of your effort. Depending on the age of your students, you may be able to put them in charge of many elements of the page and even teach them how to create the Web pages.

Posting Ideas for Classes

- Overview of the class mission statement and class goals
- Student projects: writing, poetry, artwork, math problems, science experiments, multimedia presentations
- Units of study designed by the teacher which might include a bibliography of literature read, resources, activities, Internet resources, films shown, and a timeline of instruction
- Information about the teacher: educational training, experience, philosophy of education, picture
- Featured student of the week
- Favorite URLs for sites the class likes to visit
- Homework assignments, spelling lists, reading assignments
- Dates of field trips and permission forms to be printed out and returned signed for permission
- Calls for volunteers to help in the classroom
- Lists of materials needed for upcoming projects
- Class awards and contests

3 Planning Pages

- Conference schedules
- Best times to call the teacher
- E–mail address for reaching the class/teacher

The following reproducible page will help you plan for the content of your Web pages. Use one of these pages for each Web page you create.

Once you and your class have established the topics you want to include in your page, it is time to go visit other online classroom pages and see some of the creative ways they are using the Net. Carefully examine the styles of the pages and note the spirit of each.

Teachers who are creating Web pages to encourage student learning deserve a lot of credit. By beginning to plan and learning to write your own pages, you are changing the ways educators use technology to enhance student achievement. Congratulations on your willingness to take a risk and learn a new skill which can benefit your students! It is also valuable to show the global community how students are being educated in our local communities.

3   Planning Pages

Planning Class Home Pages

page address:_____.html

Title of Page:_____

purpose of page

graphics to include

Topic:	Links:	Responsible Person:

3 Planning Pages

Write a paragraph about the class:

Class Mission Statement:

114

3   Planning Pages

Copper Hill Elementary School, Ringoes, NJ
http://www.teachercreated.com/books/3880

This group of kindergarten teachers worked together to create a friendly and usable Web page for the parents of the students in all of their classes. One thing to remember is that each teacher on a team may have certain strengths—one may be good with content and organization, one may be able to draw the graphics or find appropriate ones in a clip art collection, and one may be the techno-guru who already knows HTML and agrees to keep the pages updated on the Web. Working with others and separating the duties and responsibilities of a Web page is an option that lends itself well to the grade-level group.

3 Planning Pages

The page I think would be most meaningful to parents of prospective kindergarten students at this school is the "Take a Tour" page. This page contains thumbnails of important spots in the classrooms, and, when clicked on, are presented as full-size pictures. What better way to soothe a new student's fears than to show them the exciting areas in the classroom, and the tour even includes a shot of the all-important playground!

Take a Tour

Click on the thumbnails to enlarge pictures.

3 Planning Pages

Nathaniel H. Wixon Middle School: Technology Support Page
http://www.teachercreated.com/books/3880

HOME WIXON WAVES LUNCH MENU CALENDAR COMPUTER HELP SUBJECT HOTLISTS CONTACT US CLASS PROJECTS

Some Technology Terms:

Database: A program that helps you manage large collections of information. You can use a database to store, sort, and easily find information.

Multimedia: A powerful blend of text, graphics, sound, animation, and video on your computer. Multimedia is an effective way of communicating information. Multimedia is used in games, business presentations, interactive tutorials, and information kiosks. **See Presentation, below.**

Presentation: PowerPoint is a program for making presentations. A presentation has a number of slides that have information to teach an audience about a topic. PowerPoint presentations can be **multimedia** because they include pictures, sound, animation and sometimes video and graphs.

Spreadsheet: A program used for accounting, budgeting, and other types of number work. A spreadsheet helps you manage, analyze, and present information. You use a spreadsheet program to make a graph.

CD-ROM: A silvery plastic disc that looks just like a music CD. A single CD-ROM can hold more information than a whole set of encyclopedias! CD-ROMs are often used to distribute software and multimedia.

Digital Camera: A digital camera takes pictures without film, and stores your snapshots as digital files in its memory. Later, you can transfer your picture files to your PC through a cable.

Scanner: A scanner looks a bit like a photocopier. It is connected to a computer and when a picture is scanned, it is sent to the computer. The picture can be saved and used in presentations, reports, newsletters, etc.

World Wide Web: The fastest-growing and most user-friendly part of the Internet that lets you see text, pictures, sound, and even video. Many groups, companies, and individuals provide "pages" of free information on the WWW.

This page was created by the instructional technology specialist at this middle school to reinforce the vocabulary that she is teaching in conjunction with the classroom projects. The vocabulary words are also links to pages which illustrate the concept. This page serves a dual role as a review for students and as a review for the teachers, some of who are just learning, too. This type of original information is a wonderful addition to any school or classroom Web page, since it is tailored to fit the needs of your specific school or grade level curriculum.

3   Planning Pages

Mrs. Michaelsen's Third Grade Class: Writing Projects, Tempe, AZ

http://www.teachercreated.com/books/3880

We have been watching the Olympics and setting goals. We also have been reading The Magic School Bus Series by Joanna Cole. Here is what happens when the two ideas get together.

The Magic School Bus at the Olympics

It was another one of those days. We were studying the Olympics this time. But we didn't have books so Ms. Frizzle had promised to bring us to the library. We were all bored, but the Frizz had made up her mind.

Mrs. Michaelsen works with a graduate student to help her post student work on the Internet. Her classroom pages include stories, poems, reports, and illustrations drawn by the students, with a little introduction to the unit supplied by the teacher.

3 Planning Pages

Mrs. Dickinson's Second Grade Class, Kamali'i Elementary School, Maui, HI
http://www.teachercreated.com/books/3880

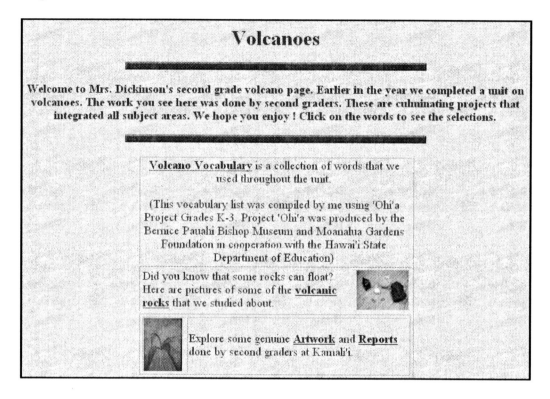

Mrs. Dickinson, a second grade teacher, includes pages that support the units she is teaching in class. Her volcano unit has links to vocabulary for students and parents to review, pictures of the rocks that were studied, and sample assessments completed by some of her students. Inclusion of this type of material will help parents understand the classroom expectations, and allow parents to help their second-graders out with a project. In addition, other second grade teachers can glean ideas from the units Mrs. Dickinson shares.

3 Planning Pages

Design Your Class Home Page

Think about the elements of the class pages which you liked best. You are encouraged to go online and visit many schools to get a good sense as to what you want your pages to look like and include. One easy way to find pages at your grade level is to go to a search engine such as Google or HotBot, and type in the phrase, for example, "second grade home page." Take notes, print out copies, and save the source codes of the class pages created by teachers and students that you are interested in. Think about the designs which capture your attention quickly and hold your interest as you visit the links.

Place your links systematically on the page. Set the links on the page up in such a way that no links near the top of the page take the reader away from your page. You want them to stay and see all that you have to offer before you invite them to try links which go to other locations.

Also be sure to include a class or teacher e–mail address so mail can be sent easily and a date of last update. If your school or district has a home page, it is advised (and may be required by district policy) that you make a link back to that location at the bottom of your page. This link lets the visitor travel to your school and then explore even more about the staff and students in your school or district.

Now it is time to get out the pencil and paper and begin to lay out the design. Once the format is created, you can begin creating graphics, saving images, and typing text.

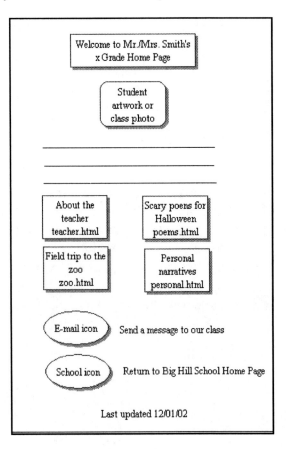

3 Planning Pages

Notice how the sample classroom layout provides you with the option to build and add to your Web presentation. The boxes with topics could be small icons or drawings done by students. These graphics might have text included so that the visitor could select to see the next link. Any design is acceptable, but some work better than others. Try out your format and see how easily you can navigate the page.

Planning in detail is going to help you as you begin to write each of your pages and link them together. A diagram of how the pages within your page structure are linked can help as you add links and makes it easier to move from one topic area to another. A class page may not have as many links as a school home page, but planning the layout of the pages is always a good idea.

One of the important things to consider as you begin to design your Web pages is the method of navigation that your Web page visitors will be using. Here are some examples of various types of Web site structures.

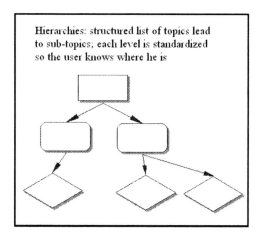

Hierarchies: structured list of topics lead to sub-topics; each level is standardized so the user knows where he is

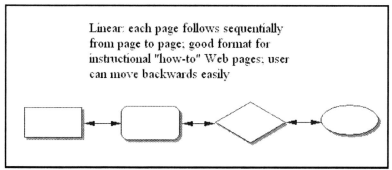

Linear: each page follows sequentially from page to page; good format for instructional "how-to" Web pages; user can move backwards easily

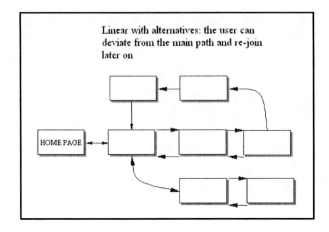

Linear with alternatives: the user can deviate from the main path and re-join later on

HOME PAGE

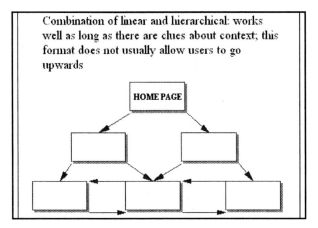

Combination of linear and hierarchical: works well as long as there are clues about context; this format does not usually allow users to go upwards

HOME PAGE

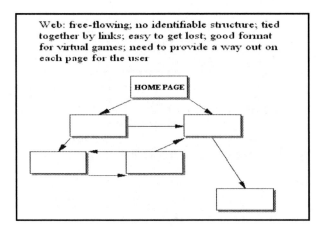

Web: free-flowing; no identifiable structure; tied together by links; easy to get lost; good format for virtual games; need to provide a way out on each page for the user

HOME PAGE

Part 4: Collecting and Organizing Information

Creating and Collecting Graphics

At this stage of page development you have planned the content of your page and the design you would like to achieve. It is time to begin to collect and create graphics, as well as get your students excited about producing some creative writing to be shared. The excitement will continue to grow as you work on the development of the pages.

To keep yourself organized as the information accumulates, create a folder on your computer and save all the digital files in one place. The easiest way to write your Web page and reference all the files is to put everything in the same folder and directory so the browser can quickly find the information. Combining the graphics files and text files in the same location makes it easier to write the tags that tell the browsers how to display each item.

Digital copies of other text files to be used for copying and pasting into your HTML document can also be filed in a separate folder. Remember that you are preparing to publish a digital document, so there will be resources from many places which need to be close at hand as you prepare to write the coding. This coding is called Hypertext Markup Language (HTML) which will allow the information to be displayed in a browser on a computer. Hypertext Markup Language is simply a plain text file which includes tags to indicate how a browser is to interpret the information in the file and how to display it on the screen.

The combined file size of the graphics and text files will determine the time it will take to load the entire page into a Web browser. This loading time is also determined by the speed at which you are connected to the Internet. The file size of these digitized graphics can be adjusted without losing too much of the quality of the graphic, and this will allow the pages to load more quickly.

4 Collecting and Organizing Information

There are currently two common graphic formats on the Web: GIF and JPEG. The GIF (Graphics Interchange Format) (pronounced with a hard "g" like gift) is best used for line-drawn art with solid color sections and icons. To make these files as small as possible, try to keep the number of colors to 16.

The JPEG (Joint Photographic Experts Group), (pronounced jay-peg) graphic format is best for photographs. This format is composed of 16 million colors, so the gradations in the photograph are realistically reproduced on the Net. There is a compression algorithm built into the JPEG format, so the files are not overly big in size, but look beautiful on the computer screen.

It is best to keep the file sizes for the images on your pages under 50 kb. This will keep the time that the page needs to load into the browser at a reasonable length, even over a dial-up connection.

All other graphics that you want to use will have to be saved or converted to these formats in order to be viewed by your audience. If they are TIFFS or BMPS, they cannot be interpreted by the browser. See page 138 for information about converters.

Student Drawings

When asking students to create graphics with markers, crayons, chalk, pencil, or any medium, try to give them small pieces of paper to use in creating their work. You might limit the size of most graphics to a four inches by six inches card. When planning to scan pictures, be aware of the physical size of the graphics. Graphics can be memory heavy and need to be reduced from the physical sizes which are originally scanned. Also, because the Internet sees at only 72 dots per inch (dpi), reducing the dpi before scanning the image will also result in a smaller file size.

4 Collecting and Organizing Information

Student-Created Buttons and Graphics

If the students are creating buttons or other graphics to liven up the page, try to create them relatively close to the size which will be used on the page. These graphics can then be scanned, converted to the correct graphic format, and saved to use on your page. When you write the HTML for your Web page, you can adjust the physical size of the graphic by designating the width and height. The measurement unit for graphic size is called a pixel. The standard size for an icon is 35 by 35 pixels. Be aware that when enlarging the graphic by using the height and width command in HTML, the picture may start getting some jagged edges which is sometimes called "getting bitmappy."

Graphic Program Use

You and your students can create original icons and buttons by using *Kid Pix*, *Microsoft Paint*, *AppleWorks* Draw, or any other graphics program. The created graphics should be saved as a GIF or JPEG file if possible. If your only choice is PICT or TIFF (on the Mac) or BMP or WMF (on the PC), you will have to convert it to the GIF or JPEG format before placing it in your Web folder for use on your Web pages.

Photographs

If you want to use a mural or large student-created picture, a better option than scanning the page would be to take a photograph of the item and then scan the photo. Photographs scan very well and can then be resized or cropped so that the remaining picture will focus on the action in the photo.

Polaroid photos do not scan as clearly, so it is suggested that you stick to traditional photographs. Most film can also be digitally developed to a disk or photo CD-ROM. Check your local film developers to see if they offer this service. You will probably need to convert these developed pictures on disk to the correct format for Web page use.

Digital Cameras

The digital camera is another viable option for using to take photographs for a Web page. The pictures taken by digital cameras are almost always in JPEG format, so all you have to do is take the photte, import the photos into the computer, crop them, touch them up, resize them, and save for use on a Web page. There are also video capture devices (like Snappy) and computer video cameras (like Connectix QuickCam) that take single shots in a resolution that is adequate for Web page publishing.

If you have access to a digital camera, the picture is taken in a similar way to the conventional camera and downloaded to your computer. Digital cameras usually have a standard and fine mode for picture quality. The difference is in the number of dots per inch (dpi) that are recorded when the photo is taken. It is recommended that most of your shots be done in the high quality fine mode as this leads to sharper graphics to post on the Web. These pictures can be cropped and brightened after they are downloaded to your hard drive. Digital cameras are dropping in price and do a fine job of capturing action for your page. The instructions for moving the graphics from the camera to the computer are clearly explained in the manuals of each camera, and most come with image-editing software, too. A common digital camera in schools is the Sony Mavica models, which store the taken photos on a floppy disk. Although other cameras on the market provide much more resolution in the photos that are taken, even the first Mavicas are perfect for Web page pictures.

4 Collecting and Organizing Information

Having a digital camera in your school means that you can collect action shots of school activities, pictures of award winners, and class projects as they happen. The pictures can be posted on the school home page or incorporated in class and project pages. The process is easy and quick since you do not have to wait for pictures to be developed. These photos can additionally be imported into other digital documents, such as student work or school newsletters, and then printed. The digital camera provides many opportunities for student publishing with graphics.

Scanners

Many types and brands of scanners are available on the market. Some are hand-held and will read or digitize a small area of an item. Others are called flatbed scanners, and most of these have the capacity to hold at least an 8 ½" by 11" document. They have a top that lifts up like a copy machine and scans a digital image of the item. Flatbed scanners can also accommodate books for scanning, as well as flat pieces of paper or photographs. Some scanners now come with transparency adapters which allow the easy scanning of traditional film negatives and slides.

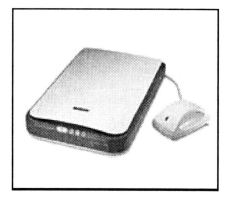

Digital images contain a record of the colors of each pixel and create files which can then be saved on the computer and used in digital documents. When large documents such as 8½ x 11 inch pictures are scanned, the number of pixels is large and therefore the file size is correspondingly large. Again, the number of dots per inch can be reduced to under 100 before the item is scanned, and a smaller file size will result. You can also choose to scan an item at a percentage of its original size using the settings in the scanner software.

4 Collecting and Organizing Information

Scanner software programs vary greatly in their function, and you will need to explore the options of setting up your program. Some programs allow you to save scanned documents in many formats, including GIF and JPEG, and if this is the case, you are able to eliminate the conversion step. Other programs are very limited in the formats which they recognize, and those graphics will have to be saved as PICT, TIFF, BMP, or WMF files and later converted to the GIF and JPEG formats which can be viewed on the Internet.

Save all scanned files on your hard drive in a separate folder so they are easily found later to incorporate into your documents. If you have a file for your Web page set up, you might want to save them there. However, if the graphics have to be converted later to a different format, it might be easier to have a graphics folder on the desktop or hard drive in which to save the files during the process of getting ready for the conversion.

Many changes can be made in the way the scanner is set up to try to limit the size of the end image file.

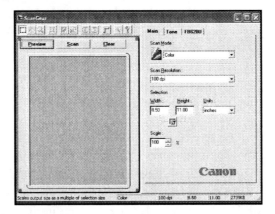

You can limit file size by

- Selecting a lower dpi number (dots per inch)
- Selecting a size that is a percentage of the original (e.g. 50%, 75%)
- Limiting the numbers of colors recorded
- Cropping the image to include only the most important subject matter
- Selecting a JPEG format (if this is available in your software)

4 Collecting and Organizing Information

Effective Graphics

Photographs

Photographs you have taken of class or school events bring the reader right into the event. Action shots can draw the attention of the reader to the page for more information. Sometimes using these photographs is the best way to tell your story.

Check on your district policy for displaying student photographs. Many districts have blanket permission slips which are signed by parents to allow student pictures to be published by the press, in school documents, but may not extend to the World Wide Web. This is an area of concern for student safety and should be discussed at your local site. My recommendation is never to post pictures of students or student names on the Internet.

Some ideas for photographs include the following:

- award winners
- school assemblies
- special night activities
- murals
- dioramas
- experiments
- hands-on experiments
- field trips
- large student-created materials

This picture shows off the mural painted by the students at North Canyon High School in Phoenix, AZ as part of an interdisciplinary unit they designed in conjunction with the Hispanic Research Center at Arizona State University.

4 Collecting and Organizing Information

Original Student Artwork

Original student artwork is a powerful method of communicating your message that student achievement is important and valued. Students love to illustrate their work, and doing so allows them to bring their own viewpoint to the situation. These original works of art can be used quite effectively to enhance student writing or liven a page of text.

This illustration of the concept of John Brown was made with crayons on an index card and scanned.

Student digital artwork is a great way for students to learn how to use a graphics program and then be able to see the original creation posted into a Web page. Digital artwork can be seen in many levels of quality and creativity.

This "wild thing" was created in *Kid Pix* in a first grade classroom as part of a math unit highlighting the book, *The Wild Thing* and converted to GIF format for the Web.

Teacher-Created Graphics

Teacher-created graphics will also enhance a page. Titles for pages are often produced as graphics because you are limited to simple text with only a small range of sizes when writing an HTML document. If you want your page title to look original or creative, you will need to turn your words into a graphic. This can be done in any graphics program, saved as a PICT, TIFF, BMP, or WMF file, and converted to GIF. Although the graphic will take a little longer to load than if the title was simply text, if the number of colors is limited to 16, the title graphic will not be too memory intensive and can display your creativity.

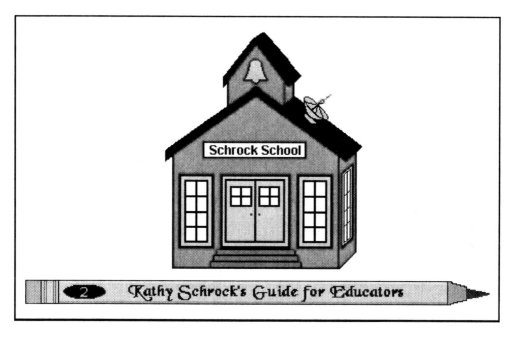

I designed the original graphic header on my site, Kathy Schrock's Guide for Educators, pixel by pixel, using *Paint Shop Pro*.

Captured Graphics

Using graphics from free graphic Web sites will help you to get started with a supply of icons, lines, dots, and pictures. Many sites have come online recently which have graphics displayed with permission granted to use them on your own pages. If you find a great graphic on one of these sites but are not sure what you will use it for, save it in a file of graphics to be used later. These files are already in GIF or JPEG format, so the conversion step is not needed. Icons, lines, arrows, dots, and so forth are small in file size, do not take up much memory, can be used often, and barely affect loading time of the page. Remember to keep note of where your found the graphic, since some of the free sites would like you to create a link back to their site as a "thank you."

An important thing to realize is that when the same graphic is used more than once on a page, the browser only has to go retrieve it over the Internet the first time. The browser quickly loads the second, third, and hundredth repeat of that graphic. Even if you resize the graphic using HTML, it will load just as quickly. So, a good tip is to use the same lines and dots throughout your Web pages to decrease the loading time of the pages.

DiscoverySchool.com Free ClipArt

http://www.teachercreated.com/books/3880/

For instance, DiscoverySchool.com has a free clipart library for teacher and student use on Web pages, as long as the following is adhered to— "Any use of clip art images on Web sites must credit Discoveryschool.com or include a link to the Discoveryschool.com Web site."

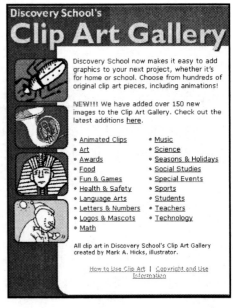

4 Collecting and Organizing Information

Free Graphics

To capture a graphic from a Web site on a Macintosh or PC, follow these steps.

- Place your the cursor on the graphic.
- Hold down on the mouse button (right mouse button on an IBM or compatible PC).
- A pop-up menu window will appear.
- Select "save image (or picture) as."
- Rename the captured graphic so the title makes sense to you.
- Select a place for the graphic to be saved on your hard drive.

Some graphics will be titled with codes or lists of numbers which will be meaningless to you. When you are saving the graphic, you can highlight the graphic title and change it. You might want to make up your own little codes which help you to remember what is in the graphics file. If you become consistent with the naming of the files, you will find it is easier later to select the right graphic on the first try. For example, name a ball, ball.gif; name a red line redline.gif, etc.

There is another type of graphic that is becoming very popular for inclusion on Web pages. This is called an animated GIF. These are little pictures that "perform" when they are loaded into a browser. They are made up of separate GIF files which are put together by a special piece of GIF animation software and create the illusion of movement, similar to the process of cartoon cells. These animated GIF files are a little bigger than the sum of their separate GIF files but make a nice addition to a Web page if they are used sparingly. One per page is probably sufficient. More than one tends to confuse the user. When these graphics are saved using the above method, they cannot be edited in a graphics editing program. If you save one of these animated gif files, you will be using it as it is. The animation can be seen only in a browser, not in a word processing program or image-editing program.

Sites Which Offer Free Graphics

The following sites have samples of graphics to use on your page and help in choosing background colors for your pages. You are encouraged to save and use these graphics and incorporate them into your page. Don't link directly to the graphics on these pages—save them to your own hard drive and send them to your Web hosting server. If your students begin to create wonderful graphics for your Web page, you may also want to publish a page of graphics to share with others.

Here are some sites that provide free graphics for use on Web pages. Links to all of them may be found at **http://www.teachercreated.com/books/3880**

Awesome Clipart for Kids

…links to kid-friendly free clipart for Web page design, reports, and much more

Back to School 3-D Icons

…a great collection of 3-D icons in all colors to use for navigation and decoration on your Web pages

ClipartConnection.com

…a huge, compiled list of links to hundreds of online graphics sites

CoolCLIPS.com: Education

…over 300 education-specific pieces of clipart to use on your Web pages

4 Collecting and Organizing Information

DiscoverySchool Clip Art for Teachers

…a free series of classified clipart graphics that are useful for Web pages and projects

Educational Clip Art from Teacher Files

…lots of collected clipart for use on your pages; includes a animated GIF section

Garden Patch Graphics

…lots of cute graphics here, especially for the elementary level

Holiday Links

…a compiled list to many holiday graphics sites; be sure to read the usage requirements for each specific site

The Icon Browser

…hundreds of cute icons to look through for those "special" places on your Web pages

Pics for Learning

…a copyright-free database of photographs, created by contributors, to use for any type of educational purposes; think about contributing your own

4 Collecting and Organizing Information

Snogirl's Back to School Graphics

…a great set of both clipart and graphic alphabets that will spice up your Web pages

Sunset Angel: Schoolhouse Graphic Set

…a complete set of Web page graphics made up of little red schoolhouses

Teacherspot: School Clip Art

…a small collection of school-related clipart to use

4 Collecting and Organizing Information

Copyright Practices

Remember that the clip art pictures that come with your commercial software packages such as *The PrintShop*, *Student Writing Center*, *AppleWorks*, *Microsoft Works*, and *Microsoft Office* should not be used on Web pages until reading the licensing agreement that comes with the software. These graphics are distributed and may or may not be owned by the publishers of the software. Their use is controlled by the licensing agreement they have with the creators of the graphics. Also, do not save and edit a graphic that you find on the Web without express permission of the owner. Do not scan for students to use on Web pages items that appear in magazines, books, or comic strips. These items, too, are copyrighted and can not be republished on the Web.

It is an easy and fun thing to capture graphics from the Web. This is a good time to teach your students about the ethics of copyright and respect for the intellectual property of others.

Converting Graphics

All graphics on Web pages must be converted into digital formats. The three main formats which can be displayed on the World Wide Web are

GIF—Graphics Interchange Format

JPEG—Joint Photographic Experts Group

PNG- Portable Network Graphics

The challenge arises when you scan a picture, take a picture with a digital camera, or create a new graphic with a paint program; it is usually saved in some picture format other than GIF or JPEG, although many of the newer programs allow you to save as GIF or JPG. Some of the other file formats include PICT, TIFF, and EPS on the Macintosh and BMP, WMF, and CGM on the PC. These formats must be converted to be viewed on a Web page.

You can see other the additional formats the software supports if you use the drop-down menu below "save as" in any image editing software program. If your program does not support GIF or JPEG formats, you will need a picture converting utility. Try to save the file in a standard format for these image-editing programs, not in the proprietary ones for the specific piece of software.

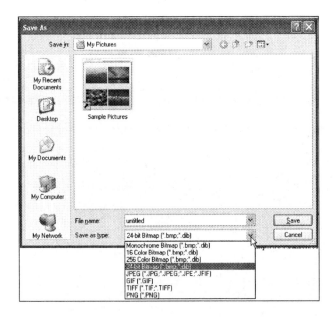

4   Collecting and Organizing Information

Choose PICT, TIFF, BMP, or WMF as the format to save as if JPEG of GIF is not on the list. There are several freeware and shareware programs available on the Internet to convert these files for both platforms, and there are commercial packages such as *Adobe Photoshop* as well.

Paint programs such as *AppleWorks, Microsoft Paint, Microsoft Works,* and *Kid Pix* can be used to:

- import pictures which have been scanned
- add text to the picture
- alter colors
- add arrows and lines

As long as the original photos or drawings are clear, they can be easily scanned and referenced in your Web page. Once the photo has been scanned in and saved as a file or a graphic has been created in a program and saved as a file, it will need to be converted to the GIF or JPEG format. After this conversion is complete, the file should be saved in your home page folder. This folder will begin to bulge with graphics and photos to allow you many choices as you create the home page.

To change the format of a file saved in any format but GIF or JPEG, you will need a "graphic converter" or a good image-editing program. Just changing the file's extension does not change the file type. Graphic converters are programs which open a graphic from almost any file type and then allow you to save the file in another format. Graphic converters can be downloaded off the Internet or purchased over the counter.

Graphic Converting Software on the Web

Your best bet to find a converter program you like is to search in one of the shareware archives by the phrase "graphic converter." You will receive hits on all types of shareware and freeware graphic programs.

One I like on the Windows side is *XNView*, which is a freeware program. It is a graphic converter/image viewer that converts just about every type of image file format (360) to over 40 popular formats.

A good program for Macintosh is *Graphic Converter* by Lemke Software. It is a shareware program that is well worth the registration fee.

If you were unable to limit the size of your digital graphic with your scanner software or if the image was taken on a digital camera, you can use the graphic converter/image editor to adjust the number of colors it consists up of and the quality of the picture. By changing the color option from millions of colors to 256 or 16 (which would limit yourself to GIF files), the file size of the document may decrease by more than half. Some student work made with markers or crayons will retain its quality if you select only 16 colors. Again, each of the programs vary, so check the manual and online help files and do what you can to limit file size and yet keep the quality you want. (Also, don't forget to purchase the shareware packages if you continue to use them.)

The graphic on the following page is a screen capture of the *XnView* screens. You can choose to limit the number of colors, brighten the picture or its contrast, resize, add special effects, and even crop using this simple program.

4 Collecting and Organizing Information

Using a Graphic Converter

Most graphic converting software works similarly to *XnView.*

- Start your graphic converter program by clicking on the icon on the desktop.

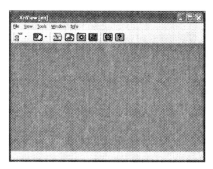

- Go to "File—Open," browse your hard drive or floppy disk and select the file to be converted.

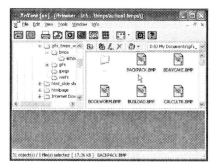

- Make any changes you wish (crop, resize, decrease the number of colors seen to reduce the file size of the picture, add text to the picture).

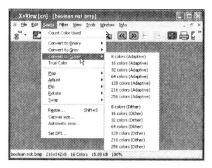

- Pull down File and choose "save as."

- Type in the meaningful name you wish to name the file in the highlighted area.

- Select the format of file you want to change the graphic to, e.g., GIF or JPEG.

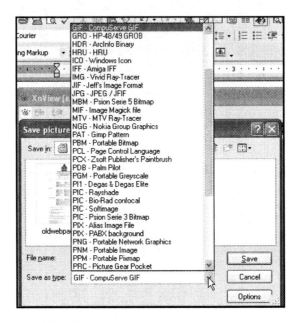

- Check that the name is as you want it and that the folder you are saving the file into is correct.

- Select save (or OK), and the file is saved in the new format in the location you have selected.

4 Collecting and Organizing Information

Naming Files

As you collect files and the number of files grow, you will appreciate beginning to name files in an orderly way. One teacher started naming her graphics with the name page1.gif and continued in that series, but then she did not know which pictures these file names represented. Simple descriptive names for files will help you remember what is in the file without opening it. You will come up with your own method of saving and classifying graphics and HTML pages.

Limit the number of letters in titles. With DOS-compatible machines, the number of letters is limited to eight with the file type extension limited to three. Limiting the number of letters also lessens the chance of a typo. It is recommended that, whichever platform you are working on, you use DOS-file-naming conventions. This means that all the characters are lowercase, there are no spaces or special characters, and that the extension is limited to three characters to indicate file type (i.e. kathy.jpg vs. kathy.jpeg or kathy.htm vs. kathy.html). This is good practice because although the pages and graphics may work just fine on your local machines, the server that you load the pages to may require these types of conventions. Examples of appropriate filenames would be redline.gif, tommy.htm, lighthouse.jpg.

Remember that the filenames returned in the browsers are case sensitive, and so all files must be referenced in exactly the same form. If the image file is named books.gif and you type in the coding for <IMG SRC="books.GIF">, the graphic will not be displayed. It is suggested that you save all files in lowercase letters so there is no confusion. When converting files, the program might assign capital letters to the name, but those can be easily changed. It is common practice to use lowercase letters for these names. For a series of pictures which fall into a logical order, you might name the graphics in order. For example, use book1.gif, book2.gif, book3.gif, etc.

4 Collecting and Organizing Information

Collecting Text

HTML pages are just simple text files with an .htm or extension. Student writing and teacher introductions need to be typed into the computer and saved as plain text to be marked up as an HTML page. Most word processors will allow you to save your final copy as a text file and many allow you to save them directly as HTML files, too. Web browsers do not recognize *AppleWorks* or *Microsoft Word* documents and therefore will not show the words if they are posted in that format. You will have to use the text format along with HTML tags to tell the browsers how to display your words.

To save writing as text and as an HTML file, follow these steps:

- After completing the typing of the document and checking the spelling, go to "File, Save As."

- Name the file by any name (best if descriptive of the information included).

- Select the folder where you want to save this document.

- Look at the small bar above the highlighted words and pull down the dropdown menu to show "text" or "ASCII text."

- Save the file with the name filename.htm.

The page will not be readable by the browser until you add the HTML tags that tell the browser what to do with the text, but this is a good start.

(If you need to reopen this file to make changes, be sure to "Save as" text again. Word processors will usually convert the text to their own file format if this isn't done.)

4 Collecting and Organizing Information

After typing your information, carefully check the document for errors. Since the items are to be saved as text and marked up with the HTML tags, it is not necessary to use normal word processing techniques for typing information, such as font changes, bolding, underlining, italics, or any other text-enhancing changes. When saved as a text file, you will only see the words displayed all in the same font and the same size. The size and some style changes can be created as your Web document is written by using the appropriate HTML tags. Graphics which you may have in your document will not appear on a Web page unless you have converted them into the proper format and have saved them separately in the Web work folder and added the HTML link to them from the text page. (Don't worry, you'll learn how to do this soon!)

Some teachers are beginning to use their class home page as a digital portfolio. In this way, each student has a Web space to display his best and most creative work. This tool can be used to access student work during student conferences, and by posting the work on the Internet, it can be shared with family members who live far away.

After the first work is posted and seen by your students, they will be ready to begin a new project and publish again. Students are just like the rest of us—they enjoy sharing their work with others, and they are thrilled when someone visits the page and sends comments about their fine work. This is a powerful motivator for them to write more and improve the quality of their work.

4   Collecting and Organizing Information

Collecting Links

Begin to collect the addresses of sites you and your class visit often so they can become links on your page. By making links to specific sites from your new Web page, students do not have to use the "bookmark" or "favorites" feature on the browser or type in those long addresses each time they want to visit a site. These addresses are called Uniform Resource Locators (URLs). Each Web page on the Internet has a unique URL.

These addresses can be divided by topic and then displayed in this categorized way on your page. Some teachers develop unit pages where they display student work on a topic and links to resource pages on the same page. Since the Web addresses can be direct links to the sites, students only have to tap on the words to travel to a new location. Working systematically, you can build an extensive resource to enhance the topics you plan to include in the year's study.

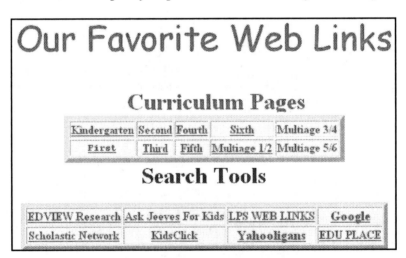

Upper-grade teachers and high school instructors are subject area specialists and can quickly collect extensive lists of resources for students to access off the class page. Links and even additional pages of information can easily be added as you find rich resources. As links change, it's easy to add new ones of fix the current ones to lead to the correct site. As the years go by, a large list of resources will help students learn to evaluate and summarize topic information as they look for primary sources and references.

4 Collecting and Organizing Information

It is suggested that you save your list of resources in a data base so they can be search and sorted easily and then added to the appropriate Web pages. Be sure to visit each of the sites selected to check that the address is active and working and also to make sure the quality of the site remains up to your standards. As you think of the many academic topics you cover during a year of instruction, you will want to add links to your page for these units and then proceed to design the additional layers to your class home page to support these topics.

Organization is the key. As you collect your files and have ideas which will enhance your page, make notes and continue to plan. Now that you have many graphics, student writing, and a plan, you are ready to begin to create an HTML document and show it off on the Web.

> Things to do:
> Find out about server space
> Test page2.htm
> Take picture at assembly
> Convert John W.'s page
>   to HTML
> Check links!!!

5 Creating a Web Page

Part 5: Creating a Web Page

Using Templates

Web pages are not created like word processing documents. The HTML (Hypertext Markup Language) coding tells the browser how to display the file which is referenced on the page. Each graphic is a separate file which is saved in a convenient location so the browser can find it and display it on your screen. The text of the page is written as plain text, but it must also be coded to tell the browser if the text is bold, large, centered on the page, where to start a new paragraph, and so forth. Creating the original page of commands can seem a large task. It is recommended that you begin with a template page and then make the changes you wish later. Templates just make the starting easier.

Students and teachers find it easy to begin to create Web pages by using template home pages. This kind of Web page is designed to have a generic format which can easily be altered or adapted to the images and information you plan to incorporate into your page. Templates are basic pages designed for the Web which can be quickly changed to include your own words and pictures. They are already coded and only need to have you substitute your words or the file names for your graphics in the spots where other words and graphics are showing.

As you begin to look at the template page and the source code, you will learn the tags which direct the design and display of the page. Many tags and examples of how they affect the display of work will be covered in detail in Part 6 of this book.

5 Creating a Web Page

Here is a sample of a completed template page as it is seen when viewed by a Web browsing program like *Netscape Communicator* or *Internet Explorer*. To see the HTML coding of a page, you must display the document source (see steps to view the source on the next page). Using this HTML text can give you a head start when you are trying to figure out how to re-create a special effect you see on the Web.

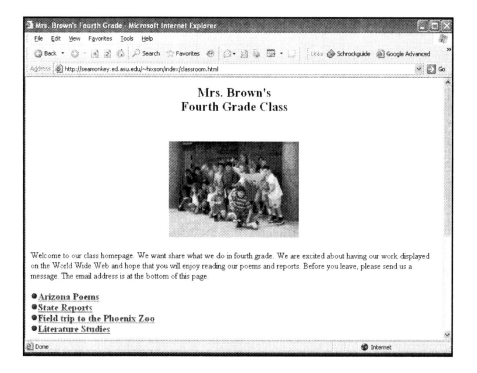

5 Creating a Web Page

To view the source of a page while you are viewing a Web page in your browser:

- Pull down "View" and choose "Source" or "Document Source."

- A text program will open and display allthe HTML coding which was written to create the page you are viewing.

- On a Macintosh, you can save the source code to your hard drive.

- On a PC, you may need to do a "save" while viewing the Web page itself to obtain a copy of the source code.

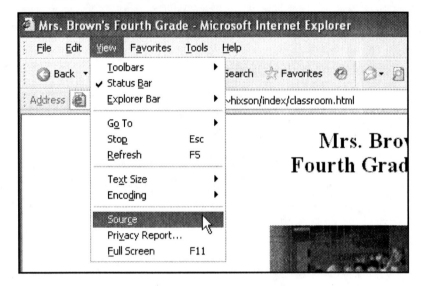

As you view the text, you can highlight and copy (and paste) the portion of the page you are interested in seeing or save the entire document for future study.

If you make any changes while you are looking at the source, be sure to save these changes and even change the title of the page so you can identify it later.

Be aware that what you are saving is just the text and HTML coding that you see in the source code, not the graphics. If you bring up this saved file in your browser later, there will be little broken picture frames or red x's where the graphics originally appeared.

5 Creating a Web Page

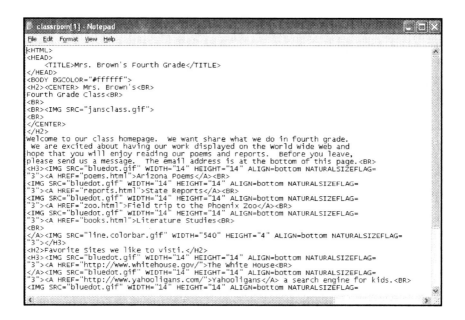

The source page will resemble the above image. All the text is surrounded by tags (which are indicated by the less-than and greater-than signs) which tell the browser how to display the text, the graphics to insert, and where to find the graphics files. Links to other pages are referenced, and an e–mail link allows mail to be sent directly from the page to its author.

You will now begin to replace the text and graphics which are located on this template page with those that you have collected. You will alter the tags to make the page look more like the one you have planned. On the next page, you will find the actual page of text with tags. To use this page and begin to write your own page, type this page with all the brackets and tags, using a text editor or word processor. If you have access to the Web, you can just visit this page at **http://seamonkey.ed.asu.edu/~hixson/index/classroom.html** and save the document source for working with it on your computer. Remember, you are only saving and typing the text file, and the graphics will appear "broken" since you do not have the graphics she used on your computer.

```
<HTML>
<HEAD>
<TITLE>Mrs. Brown's Fourth Grade Class</TITLE>
</HEAD>
<BODY BGCOLOR="#ffffff">

<CENTER><H2>Mrs. Brown's<BR>
Fourth Grade Class</H2></CENTER><P>

<CENTER><IMG SRC="jansclas.gif" WIDTH=248 HEIGHT=178 ALT="Mrs.
Brown's Class"></CENTER><P>

<CENTER><H2>Welcome to our class home page!</H2>
Welcome to our class home page. We want to share what we do in fourth grade.
We are excited about having our work displayed on the World Wide Web and
hope that you will enjoy reading our poems and reports. Before you leave,
please send us a message. The e–mail address is at the bottom of the
page.</CENTER><P>

<IMG SRC="bluedot.gif" WIDTH=14 HEIGHT=14 ALIGN=BOTTOM>
<A HREF="poems.htm">Arizona Poems</A>
<BR>

<IMG SRC="bluedot.gif" WIDTH=14 HEIGHT=14 ALIGN=BOTTOM>
<A HREF="reports.htm">State Reports</A>
<BR>

<IMG SRC="bluedot.gif" WIDTH=14 HEIGHT=14 ALIGN=BOTTOM>
<A HREF="zoo.htm">Field Trip to the Phoenix Zoo</A>
<BR>

<IMG SRC="bluedot.gif" WIDTH=14 HEIGHT=14 ALIGN=BOTTOM>
<A HREF="books.htm">Literature Studies</A>
<BR>

<IMG SRC="colline.gif" WIDTH=540 HEIGHT=4 ALT="Colored line">
<BR>

<H2>Favorite Sites We Like to Visit</H2>
<IMG SRC="bluedot.gif" WIDTH=14 HEIGHT=14 ALIGN=BOTTOM>
<A HREF="http://www.whitehouse.gov/">The White House</A>
<BR>
```

```
<IMG SRC="bluedot.gif" WIDTH=14 HEIGHT=14 ALIGN=BOTTOM>
<A HREF="http://www.yahooligans.com/">Yahooligans</A> (a directory for
kids)
<BR>

<IMG SRC="bluedot.gif" WIDTH=14 HEIGHT=14 ALIGN=BOTTOM>
<A HREF="http://www.dreamscape.com/frankvad/rours.html">
Museums, Exhibits, World Cities, and Government Sites</A>
<P>

<CENTER><IMG SRC="colline.gif" WIDTH=540 HEIGHT=4></CENTER>
<BR>

Send your comments to: <BR>
<A HREF="MAILTO:brown@mail.tempe3.k12.az.us">Mrs.  Brown's Class
(brown@mail.tempe3.k12.az.us)</A>
<P>

Come back soon!
<P>
<A HREF="school.htm">Return to our school home page.</A>
<HR>
<ADDRESS>This page was designed by Mrs.  Brown and last updated on
August 1, 2002.</ADDRESS>
</BODY>
</HTML>
```

After you have saved the source code from the template page or typed the information, save it into your working folder and name it as your own. It is suggested that you use your last name in lowercase letters and then add dot htm, for example, yourname.htm. By changing the name of the template, there will be no confusion with the original copy at a later date. Now you are ready to make changes to the page and incorporate your own words and graphics.

As you examine the coding, you see that all codes are surrounded by brackets that look like the "greater than" (opening bracket) and "less than" (closing bracket) signs. Any information between brackets will not be displayed on the screen when viewing the page in a Web browser. They are the simply the commands or tags which tell the browser how to display each word or graphic.

5   Creating a Web Page

Some of the tags have similar tags at the end of a line of text. Notice how <TITLE> </TITLE> are found at the beginning and end of one line of text. The tag is opened in the beginning and everything until the tag is closed by the foward slash is affected by that tag. This ensures that all of the text between these two tags will be found in the title bar, the bar at the very top of the browser.

Many tags operate in this fashion. For example, if you see the tag <CENTER>, all of the text and graphics will be centered on the page until the </CENTER> tag is entered. These are sometimes called "container tags" because they contain between them all the information that they affect.

The tags which need to be container tags are those which affect

- the size of headings
- the hypertext references to the URLs for linked Web pages
- the style of text or graphics
- the paragraph tag <P>, but you can sneak away without it

```
<HTML>
<HEAD>
<TITLE>Mrs.  Brown's Fourth Grade Class</TITLE>
</HEAD>
<BODY BGCOLOR="#ffffff">
<CENTER><H2>Mrs.  Brown's<BR>
Fourth Grade Class</H2></CENTER>
```

Note the page begins with <HTML>. This tag tells the browser that it is dealing with an HTML document. Every document on the Web should start with this tag.

The next tag <HEAD> denotes the top of the page. This informs the browser that this is the heading area of the document.

<TITLE> </TITLE> tells the browser the words found between these tags are to be displayed in the colored bar at the top of the browser. These are the some of the words which will be used as people search for your pages. Items between the TITLE tags do not appear on the Web page itself. Choose the information for your title tags carefully, however, because this information is what is saved when people save a bookmark of your page or receive it as a hit when searching.

<BODY BGCOLOR ="#ffffff"> instructs the browser to make the background of this page white. If there is no background color noted, the page will usually default to gray. Other colors can be set for the background, and an extensive list of the codes can be found at a site called ColorMaker.
(http://www.teachercreated.com/books/3880)

At this site you can view the colors on the computer screen and see complementary colors to use for text and links. The next few pages show you the codes to use to obtain your color(s) of choice.

Black	#000000
Blue	#0000FF
Blue Violet	#9F5F9F
Bright Gold	#D9D919
Bronze	#8C7853
Bronze II	#A67D3D
Brown	#A62A2A
Cadet Blue	#5F9F9F
Cool Copper	#D98719
Copper	#527F76
Copper	#B87333
Coral	#FF7F00
Dark Brown	#5C4033
Dark Green	#2F4F2F
Dark Orchid	#9932CD
Dark Purple	#871F78
Dark Slate Blue	#6B238E
Dark Slate Gray	#2F4F4F
Dark Tan	#97694F
Dark Wood	#855E42
Dusty Rose	#856363
Feldspar	#D19275
Firebrick	#8E2323
Goldenrod	#DBDB70
Gray	#C0C0C0
Green	#00FF00

Indian Red	#4E2F2F
Khaki	#9F9F5F
Light Blue	#C0D9D9
Light Steel Blue	#8F8FBD
Magenta	#FF00FF
Mandarin Orange	#E47833
Maroon	#8E236B
Navy Blue	#23238E
Orchid	#DB70DB
Pale Green	#8FBC8F
Pink	#BC8F8F
Plum	#EAADEA
Quartz	#D9D9F3
Red	#FF0000
Rich Blue	#5959AB
Salmon	#6F4242
Sea Green	#238E68
Steel Blue	#236B8E
Summer Sky	#38B0DE
Tan	#DB9370
Thistle	#D8BFD8
Turquoise	#ADEAEA
Wheat	#D8D8BF
White	#FFFFFF
Yellow	#FFFF00

5   Creating a Web Page

Graphic files can be referenced to become the background of your page, and that will be demonstrated on a later template. In those cases, a different tag is used that looks like the following.

<BODY BACKGROUND="bluedots.gif">

<H2> </H2>is called a heading tag. It tells the browser the size the text should be displayed on the screen. The heading sizes are H1, the largest, to H6, the smallest. Most headlines are H1 or H2. H4–H6 can be difficult to read on a screen, so use them sparingly. There are also other ways to affect the size of text.

These heading tags should not be used to change the size of text on a page. They are meant to denote levels of importance and organization similar to the ways that traditional outlines are created. They make it easy for a user to browse your page and identify the levels of information.

If you want to have "fancy text" as an opening for your page, you will have to create and save it as a graphic. Many of the headers you see on the Web are graphics, and they do present a pleasant introduction for a page. For this beginning example, we will only use text to add your name, and you can plan to create a graphic to insert in this area. When you do this, be sure to use a graphic reference tag <IMG SRC="graphic.gif">.

<CENTER> The center tag appears before Mrs. Brown's name and will not be closed until you want to no longer be centering the text and graphics. The closing center tag is </CENTER>.

 The break tag is used to get the effect of a return but does not leave extra space between the lines of text. If you want to only take the text to the next line, this is the tag to use.

<P> for a paragraph break will leave an empty line between the lines of text and should be used to leave additional room. There is now a </P> required for the <P> tag, but you can still get away without it.

5 Creating a Web Page

Begin to change the words of the template to make this page your own.

- Highlight "Mrs. Brown's Fourth Grade" in the title section

- Type in the title you want to appear at the top of your page

- In place of the title "Mrs. Brown's," enter your name, and if you want to leave the <BR>, the next line of text will show below this entry.

- Continue to replace the text with your class information.

- Save your changes and name your document, for example: index.htm

(The document must end in .htm (or .html) and be saved as a text file to show on the browser.) Browsers use both index.htm and default.htm as the default file to open. By naming your page either one of these, it will eliminate the need for the user to type this part of the URL. This comes in handy when the URL is lengthy. For example,

http://discoveryschool.com/schrockguide/

brings the users to the same place as

http://school.discovery.com/schrockguide/index.html

Remember to name only one page (preferably the home page) of your series of pages with the filename of index.htm or default.htm.

To view your changes,

- open your browser,

- go to "file" and pull down to "open file,"

- browse and select the title of your page (index.htm),

- examine the changes in your page from the original.

You will notice that the graphic for the page is not displayed. This is because you do not have a graphic in your home page folder named jansclas.gif. When you change the title of the graphic to one that is located in your folder, that graphic will be displayed.

5 Creating a Web Page

To return to your text work, follow these steps.

- On a Mac, look under the icon on the right side of your menu bar and go down to your text editor. On a PC, check the task bar for the open Notepad text file.

- Leave your browser open, and you will be able to jump back and forth to view and make changes without reopening both programs.

- On a Macintosh only, if you should quit a program and begin again and you have a copy of the page you are working on saved on your desktop, the new copy of the document source will open with a number attached to the end of the title.

<index.html45634>

If this happens, erase the number from the end of the title before you save so that you will continue to work on the same page you were working on before. If you save several of these pages with these randomly assigned numbers, you will soon be confused as to which page you want to view and alter.

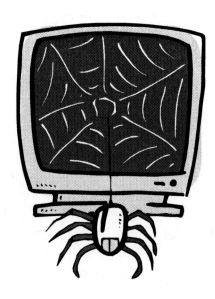

5 Creating a Web Page

Making Changes to the Template

You do not have to be connected to the Internet to work within your browser, although if you are not logged in, links to outside sites will not work. If you are online and you reference a distant site, you will be able to go to that site from your local file display.

Referencing a Graphic

<CENTER><IMG SRC="jansclas.gif" WIDTH=248 HEIGHT=178 ALT="Mrs. Brown's Class"></CENTER>

<IMG SRC="filename.gif"> is the tag which references a graphic. In the case of our example, the title of the graphic which is shown is jansclas.gif. Notice the quotation marks around the name of the file and remember the file needs to be in the same folder you have saved the HTML document you are working on. If the file is not there, when you go to the browser to view your change, the picture will not be displayed.

You are now ready to begin to change the names of the graphics to ones which you have stored in your folder of resources. It is imperative that you enter the title of the graphic exactly as it is seen in your folder. Information for browsers is case sensitive, and the files should have no spaces in their titles.

<IMG SRC="jansclas.gif"> can be changed to show your graphic by replacing jansclas.gif with the name of your graphic, "bkshelf.gif." The new line will now read: <IMG SRC="bkshelf.gif">, and your graphic will now appear in the space of the other graphic when you view it in the browser. You will also need to change the width and height tags to reflect the size of your graphic, and change the ALT tag to describe your graphic.

5 Creating a Web Page

Resizing Graphics

The size of the graphic will be the size of the graphic you have saved. You can resize the graphic on your page by adding the words WIDTH=x HEIGHT=x. These tags must be inside the image tag.

<IMG SRC="bkshelf.gif" WIDTH=235 HEIGHT=78>

Notice that the bracket is closed at the end of the line of text. You can view and see what happens to the size and shape of your graphic by previewing the page in your browser. Play with the numbers to get the exact size you want to use. Each number represents the number of pixels in the height or width of the graphic.

The bookshelf will now be longer and not as tall. Any change in the width and height numbers will change the proportion of the graphic. Make a dot graphic into a line by changing the numbers. Play with this feature until you are pleased with the size and shape of each of your graphics.

It is important to add these WIDTH and HEIGHT tags for every graphic you use on your pages. You can usually find out the pixel size of your graphic by using the graphic converter/image editor. By including the WIDTH and HEIGHT tags, the browsers, while loading the page, reserve the space on the page for the graphics, and the text on the page comes in right away, followed by the slower-loading graphics. It is also important to provide the ALT tag for every image that you incorporate. This ALT tag includes a text description of the image to allow visually-impaired users, who are having the pages read aloud to them by a screen reader program, to hear a description of the graphic.

<IMG SRC="bkshelf.gif" HEIGHT=58 WIDTH=68 ALT="Picture of bookshelf">

<CENTER><H3>Welcome to our class home page</H3>

We want to share what we do in fourth grade. We are excited about having our work displayed on the World Wide Web and hope that you will enjoy reading our poems and reports. Before you leave, please send us a message. The e–mail address is at the bottom of this page.</CENTER><P>

5 Creating a Web Page

The next section of the page needs only to be deleted and replaced with your text. If it is important to break a line at a certain place, as in poetry, you will want to write in a <BR> tag at the end of each line.

<IMG SRC="bluedot.gif" WIDTH=14 HEIGHT=14 ALIGN=BOTTOM>
<A HREF="poems.html">Arizona Poems</A>

<IMG SRC="bluedot.gif" WIDTH=14 HEIGHT=14 ALIGN=BOTTOM>
<A HREF="reports.html">State Reports</A>

<IMG SRC="bluedot.gif" WIDTH=14 HEIGHT=14 ALIGN=BOTTOM>
<A HREF="zoo.htm">Field Trip to the Phoenix Zoo</A>

<IMG SRC="bluedot.gif" WIDTH=14 HEIGHT=14 ALIGN=BOTTOM>
<A HREF="books.htm">Literature Studies</A>

<IMG SRC="colline.gif" WIDTH=540 HEIGHT=4 ALIGN=BOTTOM>

Aligning Text with Graphics

Before each entry you see an image reference to a blue dot <IMG SRC="bluedot.gif" WIDTH=14 HEIGHT=14 ALIGN=bottom>. The size of the dot is noted at 14 by 14, and the dot is "aligned" to line up with the bottom of any text which is beside it.

When you are aligning a graphic with text, you can choose to have the graphic align to the top, middle, or bottom of the text. If you want a graphic to be next to a large block of text, you can use the "align=right" or "align=left" tags which place the graphic either to the left or right of a block of text.

5 Creating a Web Page

Local Links

<A HREF="filename.htm">

This section of the page is a list of local links. These links are made to other pages of HTML text which are kept in your Web page folder. The topics are just samples and can be changed to fit with your student projects and writing. Here's an example.

<A HREF="poems.htm">Arizona Poems</A>

When making a reference to a file in your folder, you only need to include the name of the file. If the file were in another folder, you would have to include the path to the folder for the browser to find the file. Therefore, poems.htm is the name of a file with poems which you will be trying to open.

Between the <A HREF="filename.htm"> at the beginning of the reference and the </A>, all of the words that appear are the ones that are highlighted on the screen and create the link. The close of the </A> (anchor) command will end the link and stop the change of word color and underlining.

In this particular set of coding, the blue dot is not a link to the page. To change the coding of the page to include the blue dot in the information which is interactive, you only have to reference the source of a new page before the GIF reference. Now, since the <A HREF> reference is before the blue dot, the dot is included in the linked information.

<A HREF="poems.htm"><IMG SRC="bluedot.gif"BORDER=0 WIDTH=14 HEIGHT=14 ALIGN=bottom>Arizona Poems</A>

You should add the BORDER=0 attribute to the IMG SRC link so the graphic, which has now become a hypertext link of its own, does not have a blue box around it.

At this time, you can change the titles and filenames of the links to ones which you want to make to other resources within your Web of pages. If there are too many links or if you do not wish to link to any local pages, then the text can be deleted. If you need a longer list of links, just copy and paste more of the coding lines and replace the text with your page titles.

<IMG SRC="colline.gif" WIDTH=540 HEIGHT=4 ALIGN=bottom>

This line is 540 pixels long and only 4 high. If you want to include a line or another graphic at this point, just insert the title of the graphic within the quotation marks and replace the "colline.gif." You may need to adjust the width and height of the graphic to make the proportions correct for your graphic.

There is another facet of Web page design that you should be aware of. When the user is using an older computer with a monitor of a certain resolution, they may only be seeing a width of 640 or 800 pixels. The standard today is to keep your page and graphics width less than 800 pixels wide.

<H2>Favorite Sites We Like to Visit</H2>
<IMG SRC="bluedot.gif"WIDTH=14 HEIGHT=14 ALIGN=BOTTOM>
<A HREF="http://www.whitehouse.gov/">The White House</A>

<IMG SRC="bluedot.gif"WIDTH=14 HEIGHT=14 ALIGN=BOTTOM>
<A HREF="http://www.yahooligans.com/">Yahooligans</A>

<IMG SRC="bluedot.gif"WIDTH=14 HEIGHT=14 ALIGN=BOTTOM>
<A HREF="http://www.dreamscape.com/frankvad/rours.html">
Museums, Exhibits, World Cities, and Government Sites</A>

Again, the blue dot is used as a marker, but you can replace this graphic just as you did the graphic at the top of the page. There are many dots and icons out on the Web to use, or you can have the class create buttons for you. The graphic is replaced by deleting the name of the graphic within the quotation marks and inserting the name of another GIF or JPEG file.

5   Creating a Web Page

Referencing a Site Not at Your Location

<A HREF="http://www.server.com/filename.htm">Name of site here</A>

To reference the link to a site which is not in your folder, you need to include the entire URL. You begin the reference the same way, <A HREF=, and then include all the folders and page names. After the reference is listed, the words before the close </A> are all highlighted and underlined. They will be bright blue by default in the browser.

Setting Up a Mail-to Link

<P>

Send your comments to:

<A HREF="MAILTO:brown@mail.tempe3.k12.az.us">Mrs.Brown's Class (brown@mail.tempe3.k12.az.us)</A>

This is the location of a link to the mailbox of Mrs. Brown. Notice how the same beginning is used to reference a site but that instead of a reference to a Web site (http://), the link is <A HREF="mailto:>, and the e–mail address of the person is included. When this link is posted on a page and a visitor selects this link, the user's e-mail program is launched and then they can send a note to the author of the page. It is important to make sure the e–mail address also appears on the screen for those users who cannot launch mail from within the browser and will be sending e–mail via another program. This link is your link to the rest of the world. You will want to have a way for you and your class to receive feedback on the information you have posted and answer questions by your visitors.

You can select the words which you want to use as the link and then place the e–mail reference in the correct place. If you wanted a mail graphic at the beginning of the line and wanted to link that as well as the words, you would have the mail reference before the image reference.

<A HREF="mailto:kathy@kathyschrock.net"><IMG SRC="mailbox.gif"ALT="mailbox picture" HEIGHT=35 WIDTH=35 BORDER=0>Kathy Schrock (kathy@kathyschrock.net)</A>

5 Creating a Web Page

Creating a New Page

When you are ready to make a new blank page for additional pages, follow these steps.

- Go to the top of the Web page you are working on.
- Copy all of the beginning tags at least through the BODY tag of the page.
- Open a blank page in your text program.
- Paste the information on the new page.
- Begin the process of changing, cutting, and pasting information as you want it to appear on the page.
- Remember that your work can be viewed in your browser.

If you plan to create several pages and want them all to have the same background color and similar navigation, then making your own template will save you time and keep all of your pages easy to use.

On the following page is another template which shows a class list of students under which there is an individual page for each student. This page represents a portfolio of student work. The table setup is included in the document source code of the page.

This page can be modified with your information, such as your student names and links to their pages. Feel free to alter the page in any way which will make this page more like your original plan for your Web pages. This suggestion is included to illustrate how each student could be responsible for his own writing and the information he completes and posts. Some schools even use a rubric to evaluate the quality of pages created by students before they are posted on the Web.

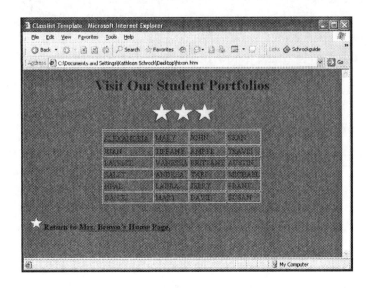

The source code for this page is a little different from the first template. You will notice that the background is a different color. The text on this page is navy blue instead of the normal black, and that had to be documented also. Look over the HTML coding shown here and on the following pages.

```
<HTML>
<HEAD>
<TITLE>Classlist Template</TITLE>
</HEAD>

<BODY TEXT="#00008C" LINK="#000094" ALINK="#730000"
VLINK="#338A68" BGCOLOR ="#C6EFF7">

<CENTER><H1>Visit Our Student Portfolios</H1></CENTER>

<CENTER><IMG SRC="yellowstar.gif" WIDTH=43 HEIGHT=42>
<IMG SRC="yellowstar.gif" WIDTH=43 HEIGHT=42>
<IMG SRC="yellowstar.gif" WIDTH=43 HEIGHT=42>
</CENTER>
<BR>
```

```
<FONT SIZE=5>
<CENTER>

<TABLE BORDER=1 CELLPADDING=1 WIDTH="100%"HEIGHT=160>
<TR>
<TD><A HREF="alexandria.htm">ALEXANDRIA</A></TD>
<TD><A HREF="mary.htm">MARY</A></TD>
<TD> JOHN </TD>
<TD>SEAN</TD>
</TR>

<TR>
<TD>JUAN</TD>
<TD>TIFFANY</TD>
<TD> AMBER</TD>
<TD>TRAVIS</TD>
</TR>

<TR>
<TD>PATRICK</TD>
<TD>VANESSA</TD>
<TD>BRITTANY</TD>
<TD>AUSTIN </TD>
</TR>

<TR>
<TD>SALLY</TD>
<TD>ANDREA</TD>
<TD>YARI</TD>
<TD>MICHAEL </TD>
</TR>

<TR>
<TD>NEAL</TD>
<TD>LAURA</TD>
<TD>JERRY</TD>
<TD>FRANK</TD>
</TR>
```

```
<TR>
<TD>DANIEL</TD>
<TD>MARY</TD>
<TD>DAVID</TD>
<TD>SUSAN</TD>
</TR>

</TABLE>
</CENTER>
</FONT>
<BR>

<B><IMG SRC="yellowstar.gif" WIDTH=28 HEIGHT=28 ALIGN=bottom>
<FONT SIZE=4>
Return to <A HREF="class.htm">Mrs.  Brown's Home Page</A>
</FONT>
</BODY>
</HTML>
```

The coding is lengthy, but that is due to the fact it is linking to twenty-four students on a grid. Only the first two student page has been referenced as links. To link all the other students, the same procedure should be followed. It is suggested that you name the pages with lowercase first names (john.htm) and if there are two of the same name, the final letter of the last name can be inserted.

Coding the Text Colors and Background Color or Graphic

```
<BODY TEXT="#00008C" LINK="#000094" ALINK="#730000"

VLINK="#338A68" BGCOLOR="#C6EFF7">
```

This coding tells the colors of the text on the page. Text does not have to be black, and this is the place where you must tell the browser how to display it.

5 Creating a Web Page

Links that are made on the page do not have to stay the default blue color, and you can select the colors you want them to display. However, if you are using a light background color or graphic, try to keep the text color, visited links, and active links the default colors of the browser. Changing these colors sometimes confuses the user.

LINK controls the color of the normal, unfollowed links. ALINK controls the color of an activated link that has been pressed but not yet released.

VLINK controls the color of the visited links.

In most cases the links will return to the LINK color after a period of time which is designated in the browser setup. Many colors can be selected and listed to replace these codes. Possible colors and matching link codes can be found near the beginning of this chapter. Pay close attention to the colors and how they display against the backgrounds you have selected. Working with a variety of colors can be fun and creative, but the main purpose of the page is to make it easy to navigate, so remember to make it readable.

Although we used BGCOLOR="#C6EFF7" to make a blue backgropund, we could have used a graphic image as the background. The coding would then have looked like this: BACKGROUND="filename.jpg" which includes the reference to a graphic file. Even though these graphic files used as background images are small in size, the browser automatically repeats the color sample in a tile-like fashion across and down the entire page. If you want to have a graphic background instead of a solid color, put the file in your directory of images. It is not a good idea to reference a graphic from another site. This causes undue burden on that site's server as well as using precious Internet bandwidth. Section 4 included information about Web sites to visit for free Web page graphics and backgrounds.

5 Creating a Web Page

Setting Up a Table

```
<TABLE BORDER=1 CELLPADDING=1 WIDTH="100%" HEIGHT=160>
<TR>
<TD><A HREF="alexandria.htm">ALEXANDRIA</A></TD>
<TD><A HREF="mary.htm">MARY</A> </TD>
<TD> JON </TD>
<TD>SEAN</TD>
</TR>
```

Working with tables has many advantages, and most of them involve the best use of page space. Only in tables can you create the illusion of columns or place sections of text side by side. Tables must be set up correctly to work on most browsers.

<TABLE> indicates that a table is beginning. The table setup will continue until a close table tag is entered, </TABLE>.

<BORDER=1> indicates there is to be a border showing around the table, and the number tells the width (in pixels) of the border. Tables can be displayed with no border, and then the page looks just like the words and pictures are listed in columns. In that case, you need to use the HTML code of BORDER=0.

<CELLPADDING=1> This code determines the amount of space between the edges of the cell and its content.

<TR> </TR> defines a table row. If you want to have four entries on a line, then there are four table data <TD> entries between the <TR> and the </TR>. All four names will appear in one row of the table,

For example,

```
<TR>
<TD>PATRICK</TD>
<TD>VANESSA</TD>
<TD>BRITTANY</TD>
<TD>AUSTIN</TD>
</TR>
```

<TD> </TD> defines the cell in which the table data or graphic is located.

5   Creating a Web Page

WIDTH="100%" tells the browser to spread the table across the entire browser page, whatever the current width on the user's screen is currently opened to.

<HEIGHT=160> is telling the browser to make all of the cells 160 pixels high.

Entering Your Students

```
<TR>
<TD>
<A HREF="alexandria.htm">ALEXANDRIA</A>
</TD>
<TD><A HREF="mary.htm">MARY</A> </TD>
<TD>JON</TD>
<TD>SEAN</TD>
</TR>
```

Notice how the reference to the Web page for Alexandria and Mary are listed before their names and the </A> comes after their names. This will highlight and underline her name and create an active link to their own pages. The next job is to create separate pages for each student and reference them from the table on this page. If you need more than the twenty-four cells created here, just copy and paste another row of cells, and you will have twenty-eight spaces for names.

Another useful HTML function to learn is the one that allows you to create lists within your HTML page. These tags are discussed in the section at the end of the book dealing with HTML tags (page 185).

Collect the Source Code of Your Favorite Sites

As you visit school pages around the world and find examples of formats and page setups you might want to incorporate into your page, save the source code of the pages. Since everyone on the Web is learning from each other, it has long been the practice of Web developers to examine how another person created a certain effect on a Web page. By viewing the source code of the page, you can cut and copy the coding used by another page creator.

5   Creating a Web Page

Be careful to use the coding only to learn how to create an effect and not take the words of someone else. You are only learning from this code so that you can later apply the technique to your own page.

For example, if you want to put a border around a graphic you have created and you don't know what the code is to do that, you can view a page that has a graphic with a border and save the source. As you read through the source, you will find the line or lines of text which tell the browser to show a border around the graphic. Make a copy of that bit of text and paste it into your page. Just add the reference code to your graphic, and you now will have a the border. This method is a good way to begin learning how to create certain effects and how to read HTML files.

Even though it seems that filling in the template is a foolproof method of creating a page and getting started, there will be glitches in the system. You will need to be patient as you go though the steps to find out why a certain coding is not yielding the decided results.

Open a local file on your browser this way.

- Open your browser.
- Pull down the File menu.
- Select "Open File."
- Look around your computer for your "front" home page yourname.htm.
- Your page will load on the screen.

If the page does not open, check that you have added .htm to the title, that there are no spaces in the title, and that this is a text document and was not saved as a word processing document in its proprietary format. Remember, the browser can read only text documents.

Troubleshooting

If a Graphic Does Not Appear on the Page

When graphics are not found or cannot be read by the browser, a box will appear on your screen with a torn document in the center or a box with a question mark will appear. The box represents the location where you have written the HTML code to insert the graphic. When the user gets this sign it means that either the graphic file cannot be found at the location you have directed, or there is a problem with the graphic file.

INQUIRING EDUCATORS WANT TO KNOW:

TEACHERQUESTS FOR TODAY'S TEACHERS

Kathy Schrock (kathy@kathyschrock.net)

If it does not show up, you can try the following.

- Check that the title of the graphic is EXACTLY the same as the file name, including the use of upper and lower case letters

- Check that the graphic is saved in the folder with your other graphics and that your HTML coding leads to this folder

- Even though you have named the graphic.gif or graphic.jpg, it may not have been converted from another format. Open the graphic in a graphic converter program and take note of the format the converter tells you the graphic is saved in. Renaming the graphic does not change the format, so you need to follow the conversion process in the software program to convert it, and then save the gif or jpeg to your folder.

5   Creating a Web Page

- Sometimes you cannot identify the problem even though it is obviously there. HTML code can be overwhelming to read at times. When this happens, go to a graphic reference which is working and copy the code and paste it in this troublesome place. Then enter the correct graphic name over the other, copied name. Usually this will work to correct any typos or HTML errors that you may have in the page.

- If you need to, find a friend who is HTML-literate who will look carefully at your page and try to find the problem. As you can tell with all the codes you have to enter, it is very easy to leave something out or have an extra space which can cause a page or graphic to not display.

Checking Links to Pages on Your Site

As you view each page of your newly created Web site, you will notice the titles you coded to be links to other pages in your site are highlighted. Test each of these links to see if the path is correct and the corresponding Web page displays. You must check all the internal links carefully. As you visit each page, make note of any graphic which is not working or any links which take you to a dead end. Those problems will need to be addressed and fixed before you go live.

If a link to another page in your collection will not open, it is time to problem solve.

First, check that you have referenced the page exactly as it is titled in your folder. The name must have no spaces in the title. Any letters which are capital must be entered that way, and the ending must include .htm

Open the page in a text editor to double-check that the page was saved in "text" format with an .htm extension. If the page will not open, you may have accidentally saved the text in your word processer's format, and it cannot be read by the browser.

Carefully look at the way you have designated the path to the linked page. If this document is not in the same folder with your home page, a specific path to the document must be listed in the address, beginning with the folder where the home page is saved. It is suggested that these documents be saved in the same folder so that this linking is not so difficult. Also, when the pages are posted to a server to be displayed on the Internet, all the folders must be sent over to the server and duplicated in that setup, in the exact same file structure. You are less likely to have errors if the organization is simplified.

Check that the address of the other page exists. You may have created your home page and planned to create another page to link to but not completed that task. If there is not a page listed in the folder, the link will not work.

Remember that any changes you make to correct problems must be re-saved as text documents.

Checking Links to Other Sites

To have a home page that is useful for you and others, it is important that your links to other sites are verified and then checked on a regular basis. You can try these links if you are logged into the World Wide Web and your browser is loaded. Open the "local file" and your page. After the page is displayed, you can now go from your page to any other site on the Internet which you have addressed on your page. Try out each link to be sure that you have the correct address and have entered it correctly in your HTML document.

If the connection does not open, try the following.

Check that the address is entered exactly as it appears at the site. If necessary, open the site by typing the address into your browser location bar and visit the site. Copy the address from your browser display and then paste the address in your HTML text document in the appropriate place.

Sites often move, so if the address you have entered is not working, it could signal that the site has been moved or deleted. Try to find the site again using a search engine and then correct the address in your Web pages.

5 Creating a Web Page

Again, when you type URLs into browsers they must be case sensitive, and not include spaces, so double-check that the address in your HTML document follows the rules for addressing sites. You must include the http:// inside the quotation marks after the <A HREF=, and there must be a close bracket at the end of the line of code >. Also check that you have the close A after the words you want to highlight so the link can be found, </A>.

A sample link should look like this:

<A HREF="http://kathyschrock.net/index.htm">Kathy Schrock's Home Page</A>

Notice that some pages end in html and others end in htm. If this ending is not entered exactly as you see it at the site, the page will not be found.

When everything is working and you are pleased with the presentation of your material, you are ready to post your page to a server and display it to the world. Information on how to move the pages over from your computer to the Web server where your pages are hosted will be covered in the next chapter.

Congratulations!

You are now well on the road to publishing your class home page. The more you play with the coding, adjust the size of graphics, add links, create new pages, and create new effects, the more comfortable you will become with coding the HMTL by hand.

Web Page Editors

It is no longer necessary to learn HTML in order to produce a Web page. If you want to create Web pages but are not thrilled about learning HTML, Web page editors are extremely helpful tools which can help you quickly create your home pages. These programs allow you to put your text and graphics into place without having to type or even know HTML codes. There are many levels and styles of Web editors, so it might be wise to visit a few of the Web sites listed here and use the demonstration copies before you make a decision to purchase one.

Suggested Web Page Editors

URLs may be found at **http://www.teachercreated.com/books/3880**

The two mainstream Web page editors on the Windows side are Microsoft's *Front Page* and Macromedia's *Dreamweaver*. These are full-featured programs that allow the user to create all types of special effects and take full advantage of the current technologies available on the Web. These programs are full-featured and there are plenty of tutorials and books available to help you learn them. Dreamweaver is available for both Macintosh and Windows platforms, but FrontPage is only available for machines running Windows. A simple HTML editor called *Netscape Composer* comes with the *Netscape Communicator* suite of tools and can be a good choice for teachers.

There are also great Web page editors that allow you the ease of working in the page view, but also easily allow you to edit the source code, include all the tags so you do not have to type them over and over, and even can automatically check your links. One example of this type of program is Macromedia's HomeSite. It is only available for the PC.

Many of the current word processing programs, including *Microsoft Word* and *AppleWorks*, which are available on both platforms, also easily allow you to create a Web page from a completed document. The HTML coding is hard to decipher if you wish to edit something, but it is an easy way to get a series of pages up and on the Web.

There are tons of shareware and freeware HTML programs available for you to try on both platforms. Check out ZD Net's Download Site and CNET's Download.com and browse for "Web editors" or "HTML editors." You will be sure to find one that meets your needs.

5 Creating a Web Page

Additional Web Page Editors

Actual Drawing
Trial available: $59 to purchase   Windows

Cool Page
Trial available: $28 to purchase   Windows

Creative Page 2.9
Trial available: $ 25.95 to purchse   Macintosh OS 8.6+

HTML Creator 3.5
Trial available: $15 to purchase   Macintosh OS 8.6+

PageSpinner
Trial available: $30 to purchase   Macintosh OS 9/10

Taco HTML Edit 1.1
Free.   Macintosh OS 10

WedEdit2002
Free.   Windows

Webstudio
Trial available: $60 to purchase   Windows

5 Creating a Web Page

The Web page editors can assist you in writing your home page. Some editors will be very helpful in adding the tags to your text, like Homesite. If you want to reference a site, you will only have to type the address and then highlight the line and click on the button which adds the tags, such as <A HREF=" ">. This alleviates many hours of typing and makes the coding uniform. It also assures that you do not mistype the HTML coding and have to spend time searching for the faulty command.

Other editors are called WYSIWYG (What You See Is What You Get) editors. These editors have the drag and drop features of many word processing tools. You can add text to a page by copying it from a text document and pasting it onto your newly created page. Changing the size of the font is as easy as highlighting the line and pressing a button to make it larger, bold, or italic.

Links can be made by choosing the words you want to show as highlighted on the page and then typing the Web address into a form which opens from the menu bar. Background colors and text colors for basic text, links, and visited links can easily be selected from a variety of sliding scales of color or color wheels and saved into your page commands.

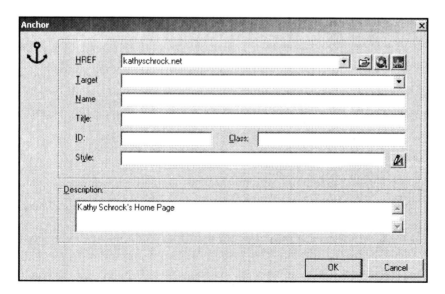

5 Creating a Web Page

Adding graphics is as easy as going to "add graphic" and then inserting the graphic you want. The pictures, buttons, lines, and icons are resized by grabbing the corners and sliding to the desired size. Even graphics which have been created in a PICT or BMP format can be inserted, and the editor will also save a copy of the picture in GIF or JPEG for you to post later.

This display of buttons, found at the top of the Homesite application, is common to many of the editors and is helpful to create the effects you are seeking.

Here you see the two versions of the same page as shown in *Dreamweaver*.

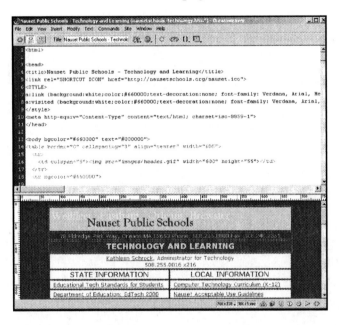

In most of these high-tech versions of the editors, you can view your text as it would be seen on the displayed Web page, and you can switch to the HTML text page and see the coding behind the screen. Some will even change the "live" page as you change the coding to show how the commands will translate when shown on a traditional Web browser. This feature is extremely helpful as you try to add your own effects to the pages and want to see how they will display.

5   Creating a Web Page

If your Web page editor does not have this preview feature, you might want to keep your browser open as you are working. You do not need a live connection to the Internet as you work, but just open "local files" and view the pages you are creating to see how they will display. You will find that they do not always display the same in different browsers or different versions of browsers, so testing is a good idea. You can have multiple browsers on one machine to use for testing.

Some features on the newer versions of the editors include the ability to add forms and tables. These features provide a simple way to begin to use columns in your page design and better use the white space on your pages. Text and graphics can be copied and pasted directly into the cells of the tables or typed in and resized to meet your needs. Additional cells in a table can be added or deleted with the click of a button, and the size of the cell padding can be adjusted as the author wishes. These features take additional coding, and it is nice to have the ability to do it automatically.

With all the pluses of using Web editors, there are a few limitations that you will begin to notice as you work to create the perfect page. As with all applications, new versions are coming out every day, and these limitations are being diminished. If you want a special look which the editor can not produce, you will still need to learn basic Hypertext Markup Language (HTML) and how to insert it into your editor document.

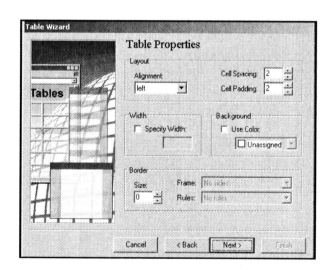

For example, some editors cannot align the text to wrap around the graphic or be to the left or right of the picture. If you looked at the text behind the page, it might say <IMG SRC="lightbulb.gif" WIDTH=25 HEIGHT= 45 ALIGN=BOTTOM>. If you want the text on the left or the right side of the graphic, you will need to change the ALIGN command to read ALIGN=LEFT or ALIGN=RIGHT. Even when you return to your editor, the text may not be moved, but when you view the page on your browser, the graphic will be moved to one side with the text next to it. Other limitations can also be overcome by inserting additional codes after the basic page has been developed.

You are encouraged to try some of the full-featured and the tag editors and use them to help you create your school and classroom pages. The editor programs will help you get the page started and might have all the features you need to reach your vision of your page.

When you are introducing students to Web publishing, the Web page editors will make the job more user-friendly. However, you will soon discover the need for a basic understanding of HTML so the pages can be modified to meet the goals of each author. Learning the basics is always helpful, and then the tools can be employed to simplify your task.

Part 6: HTML Codes and Tips

Basic HTML Tags

HTML (Hypertext Markup Language) is the language used to communicate with the Web browser so it knows how to display your text information. The World Wide Web is a hypertext information system which connects information with the click of a mouse. Designing the pathways and designating the commands is now your job as you begin to write the code.

The industry is trying to set universal standards for commands and have certain commands supported by all browsers. The current standard is HTML 4.01 and is supported by the current versions of the major browsers. As with everything on the Internet, it is a dynamic environment with many creative workers, so anything can happen. Capabilities are continually changing, but there are some basic commands that will give you a similar result with most browsers. When writing your page, it is a good idea to view it with several browsers and various versions of the browsers just to see how the look of the page might change as the different browsers interpret your commands.

In this section you will find an index of commands and examples of the results when displayed on a browser. When a tag is placed between < > brackets, the command is not shown on the screen. In some of the examples, you can see the commands, and that is only to show the command and the results of using that tag when displaying it in a browser. Most of the examples were captured from pages displayed on a browser.

The tags are divided into three categories:

- Basic HTML Tags
- Presentation Tags to create the look of the page
- Command Tags which allow you to travel to another site, page, or another part of your page

6 HTML Codes and Tips

\<HTML> \</HTML>

These tags tell the browser that it is dealing with an HTML document. These tags are found on the first and last lines of an HTML coded text page, and all other code on the page should be between the two tags.

\<HEAD> \</HEAD>

These tags inform the browser that everything contained within them is the heading portion of the HTML document.

\<TITLE> \</TITLE>

Title must be in the header, or at the top of the document, between the \<HEAD> and \</HEAD> tags. Between these tags is written the title of the page. This information is displayed on the title bar of the browser window (not as the title on the page itself. The title should describe the contents of your document, because the text of the title tag is what is saved as the Favorite or Bookmark and is also what comes up in search engine results. Sometimes the number of letters may be limited to 60 characters or so.

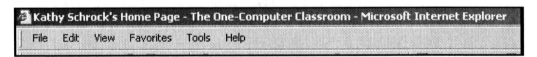

Examples of titles tags might be

- Our Class Trip to the Zoo
- HTML Tutorial and Templates
- Mrs. Brown's First Grade Reports

Weak page titles might be

- Page one
- Jim's Page

6 HTML Codes and Tips

<BODY> </BODY>

The rest of your page will be found within the body of the document, and this is denoted by the beginning <BODY> tag and the ending tag </BODY> which appears before the very last tag in the document </HTML>.

Tiled Background

Tiling a background is created by repeating a small graphic similar to how tiles cover a floor. Many of these graphics are available to copy, or you can create or scan a small graphic and then reference it to be repeated throughout the background of your page.

For a tiled background, the graphic is referenced in the following way:
<BODY BACKGROUND = "bluestone.gif">

The background can also be referenced at another site, but this will slow loading and is discouraged by Web developers. The tags for such a reference would be the following.
<BODY BACKGROUND="http://server.com/filename.gif">

Stripe on the Side of the Background

An effective method of displaying your information may include a background of one color and a stripe to the side of another. This effect can be achieved by capturing or creating a graphic bar with one color to the side and another for the rest of the bar.

Using such a graphic and referencing it as your background will allow you to have a stripe of color along the side of your page. You may even want to use this striped area for highlighting quick links to places within your site. When creating a background graphic such as this, be sure to make it as wide as the maximum resolution you think it will be viewed with (1024 pixels is a good choice), and make the height as small as possible to keep the file size small. In the sample above, the graphic could be cropped to only 1 pixel high, since, as it repeats down the page, it will appear to be a solid color stripe.

6 HTML Codes and Tips

Solid Background Color

To set a background color different from the default gray or white, you must enter the following tags within the body tag,

<BODY BGCOLOR = "#......">

For a white background you would enter this code.

<BODY BGCOLOR= "#ffffff">

The background color is determined by a combination of six letters or numbers. For a list of these codes, look back at page 156. There are 16 main colors that can be used simply by using their name, such as green, blue, and yellow, too.

Text Color

The same color codes are used to change the colors of the text. The color of the text on the page can be changed by posting this code within the BODY tag:

<BODY TEXT="#......">

For Red text you would enter this code.

<BODY TEXT="#FF0000"> or <BODY TEXT="red">

Link Color

The links are the highlighted words which will take you to another place in the page or even to another site. The link color is the color of the text which appears before the link is used. The color of the links will be blue unless you enter a color for the link.

The tags for link color are added to the BODY tag like this:

<BODY LINK="#......">

6   HTML Codes and Tips

Visited Link Color

The visited link is the color in which the words that link to another site will appear after the link has been used. You can set your browser to remember for a certain length of time that you have visited this site. When you log on the same page you have previously viewed, the links which you visited on your last visit will be a different color. This is a nice feature, especially if you are working your way down a list of resources and are not sure where you stopped after your last visit. It is suggested that you make the visited link a complementary color but different from the unused link.

The tag to change the default of the visited link is <BODY VLINK="#......">

Active Link

The active link sets the color which the link will turn as you are selecting it. This color is seen only for a short time as the link is becoming active.

The tag to change the default color of the active link is <BODY ALINK="#......">

All of the link colors, if you are changing them, need to be entered in a string within one set of brackets since there can only be one BODY tag in a document.

<BODY BGCOLOR="#FFFFFF" TEXT="#0000FF

LINK="#FF0000" VLINK="#00FF00" ALINK="#0000FF">

Spacing Lines of Text

<P>

Paragraphs are noted with the <P> tag. The insertion of this tag creates a blank line between the lines of text on the page. Text is usually typed in a block style on the Web, and this designates a paragraph break. (This tag now officially has an ending tag </P> but still works without it.)

```
The weather today will be sunny and bright      —— <BR>
and the high temperature is forecast to be 75.  —— <P>

Tomorrow the sun will shine again, so take      —— <BR>
your sunglasses and plan an outside activity.
```

6 HTML Codes and Tips

Presentation Tags

The break command denotes a break and moves the following text down to the next line. There is no line space, but you see the effect of a return on the page. This is a command which allows you to shape your text, since display screens are many different sizes, and the browser resizes the lines of text to fit the display. If you are typing a poem and want line breaks but not large spaces, <BR> is the best command.

Changing the Look of the Text

<B></B>

Bold makes any text darker to stand out from the normal type. Bold is a command which must be closed when you want the attribute to end.

<I></I>

The italic command changes the style of the text. This attribute must be closed to return to normal text.

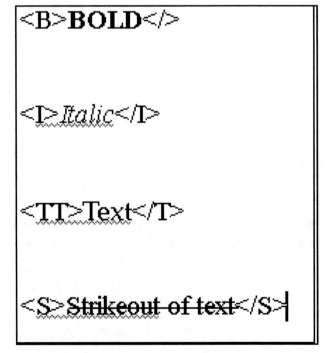

<TT></TT>

This tag changes the normal text font to a typewriter font. It must be closed to return to the normal font.

<S> Strikeout of Text </S>

Strikeout is not used often, but it is an option.

<U></U>

Underlining can be done with this tag. All text between these tags is underlined. This tag does not work in all browsers.

6 HTML Codes and Tips

<BLINK> Blinking Text </BLINK>

Blinking is a tag which should be used sparingly. A blinking word or phrase will get your users' attention, but it can become annoying.

<CENTER></CENTER>

The center tag centers anything which is placed in-between the two tags. As seen in the text capture below, the text is centered. If a graphic is included between the opening tag and the closing tag for center, all will be placed in the center of the page and equal distance from the edges of the page. This size will vary according to the width of the screen the computer is using to view the Web page.

```
                        CENTER

        Welcome to our school home page.
            We are glad you came by to
              see what we are learning!
```

When there is no <CENTER>tag, the browser will align the text to the left side of the page.

<H2><ALIGN==right> Welcome to our school home page. We are glad that you came by to see what we are learning.</H2>

The align==left tag is the default, so it is not necessary to enter it on your page.

```
                              ALIGN=RIGHT

        Welcome to our school home page.
            We are glad you came by to
              see what we are learning!
```

6 HTML Codes and Tips

Changing the Size and Placement of the Text

<H1> thru <H6>

Heading sizes are designated by the H and a number. The smaller the number, the larger the text will appear. When you want to change the text size, use both an opening and closing tag, like this: <H2>Heading size</H2> These headings should be used to designate levels of heading importance on your pages. Think of them like the traditional outline sub-headings.

<FONT SIZE = +2>

This tag modifies the base font size. For instance, if you are writing your document and you have a phrase or word that you wish to enlarge, you would surround it with the font size and a selected number to enlarge the font. After the word or phrase, the </FONT> would be closed, and the base font would return.

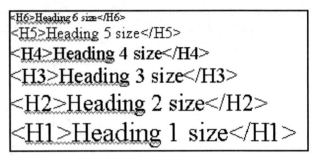

The <FONT> ...</FONT> tags enclose the text, and the size attribute indicates the size to which the font is to be changed. The values you can use for this tag are 1 to 7.

```
<H6>Heading 6 size</H6>
<H5>Heading 5 size</H5>
<H4>Heading 4 size</H4>
<H3>Heading 3 size</H3>
<H2>Heading 2 size</H2>
<H1>Heading 1 size</H1>
```

Font +1
Font +2
Font +3
Font +4
Font +5
Font +6
Font +7

6 HTML Codes and Tips

Displaying a Graphic on Your Page

<IMG SRC =."..">

There is no closing tag for the image tag.

Here is the code for the Web page to display this graphic.

<IMG SRC ="ladybug.gif">

To display the graphic, it should be in your home page folder, and it must be in the GIF or JPEG format. If your graphic does not appear when you reference it in this way, it could mean that the graphic is not in your folder or that when you converted the graphic, it was not saved correctly. You may need to open the graphic again in your graphic converter and re-save it in the correct format.

The size of the graphic can be adjusted with some simple commands to suit your idea of how the picture should be displayed. Include inside the brackets which reference the graphic the desired width and height of the graphic. The numbers you are entering width the width and height commands are in pixels.

For example, to make the ladybug larger, the coding can be changed to the following.

<IMG SRC ="ladybug.gif" width=100 height=75>

For a smaller ladybug, try adjusting the numbers again.

<IMG SRC ="ladybug.gif" width=55 height=55>

6 HTML Codes and Tips

Aligning a Graphic with Text

align=right

The <align=right> tag moves the picture to the right of the page and allows the text to wrap around the graphic, staying on the left.

Here is the code to create placement of the books on the right of the page and text on the left side.

<IMG SRC="books.gif" align=right>

The align=right tag moves the picture to the right side of the page and allows the text to wrap around the graphic, staying on the left.

align=left

The <align=left> tag moves the picture to the left of the page and allows the text to wrap around the graphic, staying on the right.

Here is the coding to create placement of the books on the left of the page and text on the right side.

<IMG SRC="books.gif" align=left>

The align=left tag moves the picture to the left side of the page and allows the text to wrap around the graphic, staying on the right.

align=bottom

Text aligned to bottom..

With this tag, the graphic aligns to the bottom line of the text, and the text will then continue under the graphic if there is another line.

<IMG SRC="books.gif" align=left>

6 HTML Codes and Tips

Creating Lists

There are two main types of lists in HTML. One is called an ordered list <OL> because it produces a numbered list, and the other is called an unordered list <UL> because it results in a bulleted list. You should usually use the unordered list unless it is important that the reader know that there is a specific sequence to the items on the list.

Lists are very easy to create.

<UL> </UL>

The unordered list opens and closes with the <UL> tags. Each item on the list receives the list item <LI> tag. There is no need to put a <BR> at the end of each list item. The browser knows to go to the next line when the next <LI> tag appears. The <LI> tag is a one-sided tag. The coding for a sample unordered list is shown below.

<UL>
<LI><A HREF="http://cnn.com/">CNN News</A>
<LI><A HREF="http://weather.com/">Weather Channel</A>
<LI><A HREF="http://msnbc.com/">MSNBC</A>
</UL>

Creating Tables and Columns

<TABLE></TABLE>

This tag notifies the browser that a table is to be created. The <TABLE> tag opens the command and the </TABLE> command is noted at the very end of the table information.

<TABLE BORDER=(a size)>
ie: <TABLE BORDER=5>

The border command is telling the browser how wide to make the border around the table and between the cells.

<TABLE CELLSPACING= a size)>
ie: <TABLE CELLSPACING= 5>)

Cell spacing adds space between the cells without making the cells any bigger. This size can be set to make the lines which divide the cells wider or narrower if you have used the border command.

<TABLE CELLPADDING=(a size)>
ie: <TABLE CELLPADDING=7>

The cell padding is the amount of space between the edges of the cell and the cell's content.

<TABLE WIDTH=(a size)>
ie: <TABLE WIDTH=800>

The width of a table is measured in pixels just as a graphic is measured. If you do not want the table to change in width when it is displayed on many differently sized monitors, it is a good idea to predetermine the size of the table. The width of the table is a design consideration determined by the monitor resolutions of your intended audience. If you don't know, keep the table size to less than 800 pixels wide.

<TABLE WIDTH=100%>
The table width can be set in percentage of the size of the page. This will allow the table to spread out to the full size of the display surface, no matter what resolution the users are seeing on their monitors. If you want the table to cover only 50% of the page, you can select that as your entered percentage.

All of these table commands can be incorporated into one long command to describe the setup of the table.

<TABLE BORDER=5 CELLSPACING=3 CELLPADDING=5 WIDTH=100%>

A sample table using a border, cellspacing, and cellpadding might look like this.

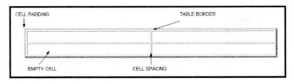

<TR> </TR>
Table row tags give the command to create a new row in the table. Each row must end with the </TR> sign. Just simply using the <TR></TR> commands is not enough. You need to include the <TD></TD> commands, too, as many within the row as you want cells across.

<TD> </TD>

Table cell data must appear between the table row tags. Each occurrence of the <TD> tag indicates a new column.

<TD BGCOLOR="#FFFFFF">

The cell color even be changed if you desire. Adding a special color to some of the cells can add a powerful effect. If a color is not set, the background color of the page will fill in the table as well. This attribute may not display in all browsers.

<TH> </TH>

The table heading creates the same thing as the <TD> command,but the information is entered in bold. Unless you change the tags, the header will appear above each column as in the example below:

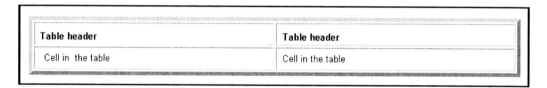

Table header	Table header
Cell in the table	Cell in the table

You can, of course, also get this same effect by choosing to put the text in a regular <TD> cell in bold.

Displaying Different Characters

Not all browsers will display certain symbols if you just type them in, so you need to enter the numeric entities in your text to get the desired result. Here you will find a few of the most common. It is especially important to use the character entities for the common HTML coding characters when you are not using them for coding (e.g., when using quotation marks to delineate a quotation, use " instead of ")

Table of Characters	Codes	Description
!	&#33;	Exclamation point
"	&#34;	Quotation mark
#	&#35;	Number sign
$	&#36;	Dollar sign
%	&#37;	Percent sign
&	&#38;	Ampersand
'	&#39;	Apostrophe
(	&#40;	Left parenthesis
)	&#41;	Right parenthesis
*	&#42;	Asterisk
+	&#43;	Plus sign
,	&#44;	Comma
-	&#45;	Hyphen
.	&#46;	Period
/	&#47;	Slash
0–9	0-9	Digits 0–9
:	&#58;	Colon
;	&#59;	Semicolon
<	&#60;	Less than
=	&#61;	Equal sign
>	&#62;	Greater than
?	&#63;	Question mark
@	&#64;	At sign
A–Z	A-Z	Letters A–Z
[	&#91;	Left square bracket

6 HTML Codes and Tips

Table of Characters	Codes	Description
\	&#92;	Reverse slash
]	&#93;	Right square bracket
^	&#94;	Caret
_	&#95;	Horizontal bar
`	&#96;	Grave accent
a–z	a-z	Letters a–z
{	&#123;	Left curly bracket
|	|	Vertical bar
}	&#125;	Right curly bracket
~	&#126;	Tilde
¡	&#161;	Inverted exclamation point
¢	&#162;	Cent sign
£	&#163;	Pound sterling
¥	&#165;	Yen sign
§	&#167;	Section sign
©	&#169;	Copyright
®	&#174;	Registered trademark
°	&#176;	Degree sign
≠	&#177;	Plus or minus
¶	&#182;	Paragraph sign
1/4	&#188;	Fraction one-fourth
1/2	&#189;	Fraction one-half
3/4	&#190;	Fraction three-fourths
¿	&#191;	Inverted question mark

6   HTML Codes and Tips

Command Tags

Linking Within Your Own Page

Creating a link on a single Web page that allows you to travel quickly to another section of the same page comes in handy on lengthy Web pages. Using this kind of link allows you to send the reader directly to the section of the page he or she wants to read next. You can put summary headings at the top of the page, and allow the user to move directly to the section they are interested in with a single click, or you can move them from the bottom of the page back to the top.

You are going to create an anchor at the place you want to be able to travel to within the page. For instance, if you were creating a list of literature books, you might want the reader to be able to jump down the page to find each title and examples of book reports. This anchor is written at the site of the book report section heading.

<H2><A NAME="snow">Snow White Book Reports</A></H2>

The tags need to be written in this order so the browser will not be confused, if you are using attributes: the header size, the anchor link, the words, the close of A, and the close of the header size. On the screen, this text is not highlighted, and it doesn't look any different from the surrounding text.

After each of the anchors is created, you will return to the top section of your page and write a link to direct the browser to travel to the location of the anchor.

<A HREF="#snow">Snow White</A>

This reference tells the browser to jump to the anchor tag you created earlier. The text that shows up on the page is a hypertext link which leads to the name reference section of the page.

If the link needed to lead to an anchor tag located on another page of the site, it would look similar to this tag, which includes the name of the page:

<A HREF="costumes.htm#snow">Snow White</A>

Linking to Another Page on Your Site

Creating a link to an HTML page on your site is fairly straightforward. The reference begins the same as all reference tags, but less information is needed to allow the browser to find the page.

<A HREF ="classlis.htm">Class List</A>

This link will take you from the page you are on now to the class list page which has been saved as classlis.htm. The tag is written this way, assuming that the document is saved in the same folder as the referencing page. This simple format of page reference assumes all of your pages are saved in the same file or on the same disk. This reference is called a "relative reference" because the path to the filename is written as relative to the current page.

If you have placed your pages in separate folders in your directory, then you must create a path for the browser to follow to find the named page.

For example, if the classlis.htm is saved in a folder entitled "school" in your file directory for your site, the reference to the link would look like the following.

<A HREF="school/classlist.htm">Class List</A>

If you have problems making the connection to the other pages or problems returning to the home page, you might want to write out the entire reference address of the page. This is called an "absolute reference."

Be aware that this link will not work if you are not hooked up to the Internet while you are testing your pages.

<A HREF="http://kathyschrock.net/school/classlist.htm"> Class List</A>

6 HTML Codes and Tips

By listing...

reference tag   http://

server name   kathyschrock

kind of domain   net

names of each of the folders on the path to the page school/classlist.htm

...the browser will now have no problem making the connection.

Linking to Another Site

Writing a link to another site on your server or to a server halfway around the world is done using the same absolute referencing.

For example, to make a link on your page to the White House for Kids, your coding would look like this:

<A HREF ="http://www.whitehouse.gov/kids.html">White House for Kids </A>

This tag would result in the highlighting of the text "White House for Kids" while making it a hypertext link. When selected, the browser will go to seek the new page listed in the reference:

- http to let the browser know that it is a Web page

- name of the server, www.whitehouse.gov

- the name of the document, kids.html

Typing "www" is not always necessary at the beginning of all URL's, and sometimes may not work if you put it there. If you cannot get to a site, try it with or without the leading "www."

Great Sites to Learn HTML

Links to all of these sites can be found at
http://www.teachercreated.com/books/3880)

Bare Bones Guide to HTML

A list of codes and what effects you will get with the different cues can be found here

Beyond the Son of Filamentality

This is an instructional guide to customizing school Web pages

HTML Crash Course for Educators

Andy Carvin's tutorial introduces you to the basics of HTML design and style.

HTML Goodies: Web Page Primer

A well-written set of seven tutorials on the basics of HTML.

Kathy Schrock's Basic HTML Slide Show

My online slide show summarizing the basics of HTML Web page design.

Kathy Schrock's List of Web Page Rubrics

My page with links to many Web page rubrics to evaluate yourself and students on the aspects of good Web page design.

NCSA's HTML Primer

A detailed list of codes and instructions for creating a home page is in this primer.

PageTutor.com: Web Page Tutorial

A chatty online Web page tutorial; the site also includes tutorials for some advanced HTML topics.

6   HTML Codes and Tips

SchoolNet's Web Page Tutorial

This online slide show's purpose is to introduce students and teachers to the basics of Web page publishing.

Setting Up a Website for Your School

This page is intended to provide a starting point for school Web page creation.

Web66: 8 Minute HTML Primer

Use this page a quick review of what you have been learning, or to keep by your computer as a reminder

Writing HTML

This is a wonderful tutorial for creating WWW pages produced at the Maricopa Center for Learning and Instruction. It gives rationale and step-by-step instructions along with links to other sites for help.

7 Showing Your Web Page to the World

Using Your Page Locally

After all the hard work, you are ready to publish your page for others to see! This is an exciting aspect and not a difficult task. There are many ways to use the page that you have created to support teaching and learning.

If you have photographs of students on the page that you do not have permission to show to the world or want to use students' first and last names on all their work, you may not want the world to see your page. However, you do want your class to see the page and use the resource links. You can do this by opening your file locally when you have your browser open and are logged on to the Internet. When the page is opened, all the links will work, and you and your students can use these resource links with ease. You can travel from your page to the Net, but no one on the Web can view your page. This feature allows educators without access to a server on the Internet to use their Web pages.

You can even set your browser home page as the HOME button on your browser so that it loads your page when you open the browser.

Setting the Home Page Address in Your Browser

- Choose "EDIT—PREFERENCES" (*Netscape*) or "TOOLS—INTERNET OPTIONS"—(*Internet Explorer*) from the file menu

- Choose NAVIGATOR (*Netscape*) or the GENERAL TAB (*IE*)

- You can see, from the dialog box, what page is currently the home page for your browser

If your local page is displayed on the browser at this time, copy and paste the address of the page and paste it in the box for the URL of the page you wish to select for the home page Close this window by pressing the "ok" button and the new home page is set. When you go back to your browser and hit the "Home" button, your newly set page should appear. If you were not on the page when you were setting the home page address, simply use the "browse" button and navigate to the page on your local computer.

Having your class page as your browser's home page provides you with some great advantages. Your students view the page each time they open the browser, re-read any work they have posted. They easily visit sites you have linked to your page to complete assignments or look for information. You are using the Internet in a controlled and supervised manner, and provisioning sites for students is important. The drawbacks are that you will not receive feedback from outsides from the page and you are not sharing your class' great work with the community.

Use Your Browser to Display Slide Shows and Lesson Guidelines

Remember to use your browser to display any information you enter in HTML and save on your hard drive, disk, or local server. One helpful feature is to use the browser to display a presentation with graphics and text. If you have a larger monitor and scan converter or a video projector, the pages can effectively be used as teaching tools. This feature of the browser will work even if the computer does not have a connection to the Internet. However, if the browser is logged onto the Internet as you do your presentation, resources which are linked within your presentation will be displayed when clicked. This allows you to use any of the resources on the Internet as a part of the lesson.

7   Showing Your Web Page to the World

Download Sites and Show on Stand-Alone Computer

Today's browsers will open and work on any computer, even if there is no Internet connection. *Internet Explorer* and *Netscape Navigator* now allow you to download entire Internet sites and save them for your viewing later. This feature creates many educational opportunities as libraries of disks containing virtual field trips and extensive information can be collected on your hard drive. Just imagine downloading and saving a tour of the White House. You could then use the tour on a stand-alone computer as a center activity, and you would not have to be concerned with the site being available or the network being down. Students easily have access to the information and yet are limited from the more risky searching they might like to do if left alone on a connected computer. You are encouraged to experiment with this feature of the browsers and see what you can do to make learning more fun.

Remember to respect copyright when downloading entire sites to use locally. Send a note to the Web masters of the sites you wish to save, ask for permission, and save a copy of the permission letter. You are all set!

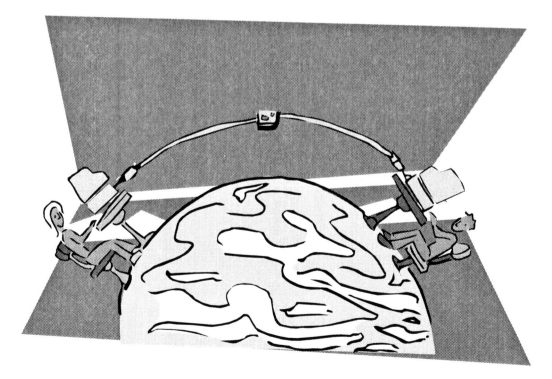

Posting Your Page on an Internet Server

Before you can post your page to a server (a computer always hooked to the Internet that is set up to display your page to anyone who accesses it), you must have an account set up on that server. Someone who administers your school or district server can issue you an account of your own if your school has a server. Districts are approaching this level of access to the Web in different ways. Some accounts are limited to only one per school, and then only the approved person is allowed to post information. Some districts expect all information which is ready to be posted to be sent into the district and posted by the systems operator. You will have to check the policy and procedures of your district or school which allow you to post to a server that is connected to the Internet and publicly accessible.

If you have a personal Internet account with privileges to post information, then you can use that space to display your class's work. Most private providers allow their customers to post five megabytes of server space or even more. When you sign up for your account, check to see if your service includes server space for your own home page. Services will charge more if the site you wish to post is commercial, but they don't change extra for posting educational material or personal pages. They may even set up a special directory for your class if you explain what you are doing with your students.

The method for posting your information may vary considerably from one service to another. You must question your provider about the best method for posting your information. The newer operating systems (Windows XP and Mac OSX) both include the file transfer protocol (FTP) or moving data from your local computer to a Web server. There are many shareware programs available for FTPing, and many of the Web page editing tools come with the ability to do this, too.

Connecting to Your Site

To use the (FTP) program, you must have the following information to enter in the boxes. To travel to the next box, you may use your mouse or the tab, but do not hit return or the incomplete information will be sent. This information should all be supplied by your access provider or systems administrator.

- The FTP host address is the URL of the server you are using and also may include your specific sub-directory

- The FTP username is the name of your account

- Password is where you enter the password for your account. Be sure to type it just as you were instructed. It is probably case sensitive and should have no spaces in it. Remember, the password may include numbers and letters in any combination.

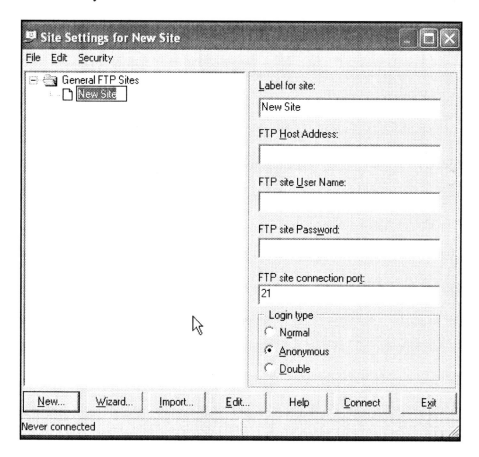

After all of the blanks are filled, you click on the "ok" button or hit return, and your FTP program will locate your account. When the software connects, the directory which has been assigned to you will be displayed.

Having an account on the Internet is a responsibility, and you want to be aware of any information posted to your account. A problem could arise if you are letting others have easy access to your account for posting. For this reason, keep your password a secret.

Creating Folders or Subdirectories

Use the FTP program to make directories on the server that mirror the ones on your hard drive. You will usually find this option under one of the menus at the top of the screen.

- Name the folder the same as the folder in your local file setup. You can also put all your files in the root directory, and, in this case, will not have to create any folders. Carefully set up your account. The files must be placed in the same relationship to each other as they reside on your hard drive.

- If you put all your graphics in a separate "graphics" folder, then on the server, you will want to make a new folder and name it graphics, just as you did locally when writing your page.

More folders can be made for larger projects. Additional folders within folders can also be created if the project is particularly large. However, keeping everything in the same folder makes the linking to text and graphics easier when writing HTML.

7   Showing Your Web Page to the World

Once you are ready to upload the files, look for menu selections like "Put Files" or "Upload Files." Look through your listed files and select the ones which need go into the server directory by CNTRL-clicking on each. When you have selected all that you wish to transfer, simply drag the list of them from your local drive to the servers. For individual files, just double-clicking on a file will send it from your computer to the server.

These programs also allow you to download files form the server and delete files from the server. Check the documentation that came with the program in order to do this.

How Your Page Will Finally Be Addressed

When your files are placed in a folder, the folder name is added to the Internet address, for example, http://kathyschrock.net/cooking/tools/index.htm

This address will take your browser to look at the kathyschrock.net server, the cooking subdirectory, the tools sub-sub directory, and in that folder, the index.htm page. You have told the browser how to find the beginning page of the series. If the lead or front page of the Web site is named index.htm, and the user enters the URL of the whole address and ends with a slash, without typing the index.htm filename, the front page will open by default.

Check Your Posted Pages for Glitches

After you have sent all the needed documents to your server account, it is imperative that you log on to the Internet, open your browser, and travel to the address of your page. Even with all your hard work to enter the links correctly and type in the names of the graphics just as they appear on the file, there is a chance that something will not show or work when the files are being viewed over the network. If there are broken links, errant tags showing up, or little "broken image" icons, go back and check your HTML code or make sure you moved all the reference HTML and graphics files up to the server.

7 Showing Your Web Page to the World

You will be excited to see the page and proud of your work as your graphics load and everything appears. If any of the graphics do not open, note which ones as you scroll down the page. Also note text that may not be appearing in the locations you had planned. Try out all the links to other pages and note any which do not work. This list of "not working" items will guide you in the process to make the page perfect.

After you have checked out all the features of the page, including trying to send yourself e–mail, you are ready to begin to make the minor fixes. Don't be discouraged; it seems that most pages have something that does not work on the first loading. Since you are at your page, view the source of the page and begin to check on the challenging points.

Check the Graphic Titles

Check that the graphic names have no spaces and that they are referenced exactly as they were saved on the server, for example, gif and not GIF.

Check E–mail Links

If you can not use the link to send mail, be sure that the link is typed

<A HREF="mailto:yourname@youraddress.com">Your Name</A>

You must have the quotation marks and the "mailto" phrase at the beginning of the address. In this type of URL, there are no slashes following the colon.

Check the Spelling, Spacing, and Case of Letters in the URL

Unfortunately, this process can be frustrating when first beginning, but soon you will become familiar with the process and know what to check and how to quickly fix the problems.

7 Showing Your Web Page to the World

Creating Traffic to Your Page

Once everything is working, it is time to show off your hard work and celebrate. If you have just posted a school page, send a note to Web66 so it can be added to the thousands of other schools on the Web. Send an e–mail to tell them to let them know your site can be linked to theirs from the school directory page.

If this is your class page or a project, notify the Webmaster for your school page so that a link can be created to help others reach your page quickly and easily from the district page. Let the community know about the page by sending the URL home in the weekly newsletter, or put it in the local paper.

Make sure to share your project with other staff members and to let your colleagues know that you would be willing to help them learn how to post a page, too. Do a ten-minute presentation at a faculty meeting explaining the process you went through to get the page designed, done, and up on the Web.

Sharing your project and topics of information on a listserv or newsgroup with fellow teachers is a gratifying way to create some traffic to the page and begin to receive responses for you and your students' hard work.

Appendices

8 Appendices

CRITICAL EVALUATION Guides for Students

CRITICAL EVALUATION OF A WEB SITE:
ELEMENTARY SCHOOL LEVEL
© 1996-2003 Kathleen Schrock (kathy@kathyschrock.net)
http://kathyschrock.net/

1. How are you hooked to the Internet?
   ___ Computer and modem
   ___ Direct connection at school
   ___ Direct connection at home (DSL, Broadband)

2. If you are using a modem, what is the speed?
   28.8   33.6+   56K

3. What Web browser are you using? _____

4. What is the URL of the Web page you are looking at?
   http:// _____

How Does It Look?

Does the page take a long time to load?	YES / NO
Are there big pictures on the page?	YES / NO
Is the spelling correct on the page?	YES / NO
Is the author's name and e–mail address on the page?	YES / NO
Is there a picture on the page that you can use to choose links?	YES / NO
Is there information in columns (table) on the page?	YES / NO
If you go to another page, is there a way to get back to the first page?	YES / NO
Is there a date that tells you when the page was made?	YES / NO

Do the photographs look real?   YES / NO / NO PHOTOGRAPHS

Do the sounds sound real?   YES / NO / NO SOUNDS

What Did You Learn?

Does the title of the page tell you what it is about?   YES / NO

Is there an introduction on the page that tells you what is included?   YES / NO

Are the facts on the page what you were looking for?   YES / NO

Would you have gotten more information from the encyclopedia?   YES / NO

Would the information have been better in the encyclopedia?   YES / NO

Does the author of the page say some things you disagree with?   YES / NO

Does the author of the page include information that you know is wrong?   YES / NO

Do the pictures and photographs on the page help you learn?   YES / NO / NO PICTURES

Summary

Looking at all of the questions and answers above, write a paragraph telling why this Web site is helpful (or not helpful) for your project.

_____

_____

_____

_____

_____

8 Appendices

CRITICAL EVALUATION Guides for Students

CRITICAL EVALUATION OF A WEB SITE:
MIDDLE SCHOOL LEVEL
© 1996-2003 Kathleen Schrock (kathy@kathyschrock.net)
http://kathyschrock.net/

1. What type of connection do you have to the Internet?

___ Dial-in access; modem speed (choose 1) 28.8k   56k

___ Direct connection; (choose 1) 56K   T1   T3 other: _____

2. What Web browser are you using?

_____

3. What is the URL of the Web page you are evaluating?

http://_____

Part One: Looking at and Using the Page

Does the page take a long time to load?	YES / NO
Are the pictures on the page helpful? NOT APPLICABLE	YES / NO /
Is each section of the page labeled with a heading?	YES / NO
Did the author sign his/her name?	YES / NO
Did the author give you his/her e–mail address?	YES / NO
Is there a date on the page that tells you when it was last updated? YES / NO	
Is there an image map (big picture with links) on the page?	YES / NO
Is there a table (columns of text) on the page? (Check the source code.)	YES / NO

8 Appendices

- If so, is the table readable with your browser?   YES / NO

If you go to another page on the site, can you get
back to the main page?   YES / NO

Are there photographs on the page?   YES / NO

- If so, can you be sure that photographs have not
  been changed by the author?   YES / NO

- If you're not sure, should you accept the photos as true?   YES / NO

Summary of Part One

Using the data you have collected above, write a paragraph explaining why
you would or wouldn't recommend this site to a friend for use with a project.

_____

_____

_____

_____

_____

_____

_____

Part Two: What Is on the Page and Who Put It There?

Does the title of the page tell you what it is about?   YES / NO

Is there a paragraph on the page explaining what it is about?   YES / NO

8 Appendices

Is the information on the page useful for your project?   YES / NO

  • If not, what can you do next? _____

Would you have gotten more information from an
encyclopedia?   YES / NO

Is the information on the page current?   YES / NO

Does up-to-date information make a difference for
your project?   YES / NO

Does the page lead you to some other good
information (links)?   YES / NO

Does the author of the page present some information
you disagree with?   YES / NO

Does the author of the page present some information
that you think is wrong?   YES / NO

Does some information contradict information you
found elsewhere?   YES / NO

Does the author tell you about him/herself?   YES / NO

Do you feel that the author is knowledgeable a
bout the topic?   YES / NO

Are you positive the information is true?   YES / NO

What can you do to prove the information is true?

_____

_____

_____

_____

_____

8 Appendices

Summary of Part Two

Looking at the data you have collected in part two, compose a note to the author of the Web site explaining how you are going to use the Web site in your project and what your opinion is of the page's content.

_____

_____

_____

_____

_____

_____

_____

_____

_____

_____

_____

_____

_____

_____

_____

_____

8 Appendices

CRITICAL EVALUATION Guides for Students

CRITICAL EVALUATION OF A WEB SITE:
SECONDARY SCHOOL LEVEL
© 1996-2003 Kathleen Schrock (Kathy@kathyschrock.net)
http://kathyschrock.net/eval/

Are you using dial-in access?   YES / NO

  • If so, what speed is your modem?   28.8k   33.6k   56k

Are you using a direct connection?   YES / NO

  • If so, what type? 56K T1 Broadband DSL other: _____

What Web browser are you using?

_____

URL of Web page you are evaluating:

http:// _____

Technical and Visual Aspects of the Web Page

Does the page take a long time to load?   YES / NO

Do the pictures add to the page?   YES / NO / NOT APPLICABLE

Is the spelling correct on the page?   YES / NO

Are there headings and subheadings on the page?   YES / NO

  • If so, are they helpful?   YES / NO

Is the page signed by the author?   YES / NO

Is the author's e–mail address included?   YES / NO

Is there a date of the last update?   YES / NO

• If so, is the date current?	YES / NO
Is the format standard and readable with your browser?	YES / NO
Is there an image map on the page?	YES / NO
Is there a table on the page? (You may have to look at the source code to tell.)	YES / NO
• If so, is the table readable with your browser?	YES / NO
If you have graphics turned off, is there a text alternate to the images?	YES / NO
On supporting pages, is there a link back to the home page?	YES / NO
Are the links clearly visible and explanatory?	YES / NO
Is there a picture or a sound included?	
• If so, can you be sure that a picture or sound has not been edited?	YES / NO
• If you are not sure, should you accept the information as valid for your purpose?	YES / NO
Content	
Is the title of the page indicative of the content?	YES / NO
Is the purpose of the page indicated on the home page?	YES / NO
When was the document created? _____	
Is the information useful for your purpose?	YES / NO

8 Appendices

Would it have been easier to get the information
somewhere else?   YES / NO

Would information somewhere else have been different?   YES / NO

• If so, why?_____

Did the information lead you to other sources that
were useful?   YES / NO

Is a bibliography of print sources included?   YES / NO

Is the information current?   YES / NO

Does up-to-date information matter for your purpose?   YES / NO

Does the information appear biased?   YES / NO

Does the information contradict something you found
somewhere else?   YES / NO

Do most of the pictures supplement the
content of the page?   YES / NO / NOT APPLICABLE

Authority

Who created the page?

_____

What organization is the person affiliated with?_____

Has the site been reviewed by an online reviewing agency?   YES / NO

Does the domain of the page influence your evaluation
of the site?   YES / NO

Are you positive the information presented is true?   YES / NO

What can you do to prove that it is true?

_____

Are you satisfied that the information is useful for
your purpose?   YES / NO

   • If not, what can you do next?

   _____

   _____

Can you get a printed version of the information?   YES / NO

Narrative Evaluation

Looking at all of the data you have collected above while evaluating the site,
explain why or why not this site is (or is not) valid for your purpose. Include
the aspects of technical content, authenticity, authority, bias, and subject
content.

_____

_____

_____

_____

_____

_____

_____

_____

8 Appendices

Bibliographic Citation Formats for All Grade Levels

Works Cited for Grades 1

For a book:

1. Name of the author.

2. Title of the book, italicized.

   Joanna Cole. *The Magic Schoolbus, Lost in the Solar System.*

For an article from a print encyclopedia:

1. Name of the article you looked up.

2. Name of the encyclopedia, italicized.

   Shark. *The World Book Encyclopedia.*

For an article from an encyclopedia on CD-ROM:

1. Name of the article you looked up.

2. Name of the encyclopedia, italicized.

3. CD-ROM.

   Abraham Lincoln. *Compton's Interactive Encyclopedia.* CD-ROM.

   Dinosaur. *First Connections: The Golden Book Encyclopedia.* CD-ROM.

For an article from an encyclopedia found online:

1. Name of the article you looked up.

2. Name of the encyclopedia, italicized.

3. Online.

   Dinosaur. *World Book Online.*

   Turtle. *Compton's Living Encyclopedia.* Online.

8 Appendices

Works Cited for Grades 2

For a book:

1. Name of the author.

2. Title of the book, italicized.

3. Date book was published.

   Neil Ardley. The Science Book of Magnets. 1991.

For an article from a print encyclopedia:

1. Subject of the article you looked up.

2. Title of the encyclopedia, italicized .

3. Year the encyclopedia was published.

   Planet. The World Book Encyclopedia. 1995

For an article from an encyclopedia on CD-ROM:

1. Subject of the article you looked up.

2. Title of the encyclopedia, italicized .

3. Date the encyclopedia was published.

4. CD-ROM.

   George Washington. The World Book Multimedia Encyclopedia. 1995. CD-ROM.

   Elephant. First Connections: The Golden Book Encyclopedia. 1992. CD-ROM.

For an article from an encyclopedia found online:

1. Subject of the article you looked up.

2. Title of the encyclopedia, italicized.

3. Online.

   Panda. *World Book Online.* Online.

   Tornado. *Grolier Multimedia Encyclopedia.* Online.

8 Appendices

Works Cited for Grades 3

1. Follow the punctuation in the examples exactly.
2. Be sure to put the author's last name before the first name, with the two names separated by a comma.
3. If you look up information about a person in an encyclopedia, that person's name should also be written last name first.
4. If you cannot find some information, such as author, just leave it out.

For a book:

1. Author's name, last name first.
2. Title of book, italicized.
3. Copyright date.

Landau, Elaine. *Sea Horses.* 1999.

For an article from a print encyclopedia:

1. The subject you looked up, in quotation marks.
2. Full title of encyclopedia, italicized .
3. Copyright date.

"Jaguar." *International Wildlife Encyclopedia.* 1991

"Washington, George." *The World Book Encyclopedia.* 2000.

For an article from an encyclopedia on CD-ROM:

1. The subject you looked up, in quotation marks.
2. Full title of encyclopedia, italicized.
3. Copyright date.
4. CD-ROM.

"Earthquake." *Compton's Interactive Encyclopedia.* 1994. CD-ROM.

"Dog." *First Connections: The Golden Book Encyclopedia.* 1995. CD-ROM.

"Tiger." *The San Diego Zoo Presents The Animals!* 1994. CD-ROM.

8 Appendices

For an encyclopedia from an online service:

1. The subject you looked up, in quotation marks.
2. Full title of encyclopedia, italicized .
3. Date you visited (proper format in the example).
4. Online.

   "Panda." Compton's Living Encyclopedia. 23 Nov. 1999. Online.

For an article from the World Wide Web:

1. Name of the author, if you can find it, last name first.
2. Title of the article, in quotes.
3. Title of the home page, if available, italicized.
4. Date you visited (see the examples).
5. First part of the http address (see the examples), in brackets.

   Schaller, George B. "Tiger."World Book Online. 16 Dec. 1999.
   <http://www.worldbookonline.com>.

   "Cheetah." The Cyber Zoomobile. 23 Nov. 1998.
   <http://www.primenet.com/>.

   "Factoids: Polar Bears." Environmental News Network.
   26 Jan. 1998. <http://www.enn.com/>.

   Arnett, Bill. "The Moon." The Nine Planets. 21 May 1998.
   <http://seds.lpl.arizona.edu/>.

8 Appendices

Works Cited for Grades 4

1. For each source listed, begin first line at margin and indent each line that follows.
2. Follow punctuation of the examples exactly.
3. If you cannot find some information, such as author or place of publication, just leave it out.
4. Arrange all sources in one list, alphabetically by first word, which will generally be either the author's last name or the first important word of the title (ignore A, An, The as the first word in the title.)

PRINT SOURCES

Book with one author:

1. Author, last name first.
2. *Title of book.* (italicized)
3. City of publication:
4. Publisher, date of publication.

   Gibbons, Gail. *Caves and Caverns. New York:* Harcourt Brace, 1993.

Book with two authors:

1. Authors, in order they are listed on the title page.
2. *Title of book.* (italicized)
3. City of publication:
4. Publisher, date of publication.

   Ride, Sally and Tom O'Shaughnessy. *The Third Planet.* New York: Crown Publishers, 1994.

Encyclopedia and other familiar reference books:

1. Author of article (if available).
2. "Title of article."
3. *Title of book.* (italicized)
4. Date of edition. (Volume and page number not necessary if articles are arranged alphabetically).

8 Appendices

Bigg, Michael A. "Whale." *The World Book Encyclopedia.* 1992.

Fehrenbacher, Don E. "Lincoln, Abraham." *The New Book of Knowledge.* 1994.

"New Jersey." *Compton's Encyclopedia.* 1992.

Article in a periodical (magazines, newspapers):

1. Author (if available).
2. "Title of article."
3. *Periodical title* (italicized) date: page.

   Bonar, Samantha. "Forecast: Hot and Hotter!" *3-2-1 Contact* June 1996: 8–10.

   Neeley, Dequendre. "Retirement complex proposed in Oradell." *The Record* 21 Aug. 1996: NJ1.

ELECTRONIC SOURCES

Encyclopedia and other publications on CD-ROM

1. Author (if available).
2. "Title of article."
3. Title of product (underlined).
4. Edition or version (if relevant)
5. CD-ROM.
6. City of publication: Publisher, date of publication.

   Garbarino, Merwyn S. "Delaware Indians." *The World Book Multimedia Encyclopedia.* 1995 ed. CD-ROM. Chicago: World Book Inc., 1995.

   Musser, Jay C. "Chocolate." *Grolier MultiMedia Encyclopedia.* 1992 ed. CD-ROM. Danbury, CT: Grolier Electronic Publishing, Inc., 1992.

ONLINE SOURCES

Encyclopedia from an online service:

1. Author, if shown
2. "Title of the article."
3. Name of encyclopedia (underlined).

4. Name of publisher, date of publication, if available.

5. Date of your visit.

6. Name of the online subscription service hosting the encyclopedia.

"Planets." *Compton's Living Encyclopedia.* Compton's Learning Company, 1996. 29 Aug. 1998 CLAMSnet.

Kelland, Frank. "New Jersey." *Grolier Multimedia Encyclopedia,* Grolier Interactive Inc. 13 July 1998. America Online.

World Wide Web:

1. Author, if known

2. "Title of the article."

3. <u>Title of complete work</u> (underlined).

4. Date of your visit.

5. <full http address>. (enclosed in angle brackets)

Clemens, Paul and Robert M. Hordon. "New Jersey." *World Book Online.* 12 Dec. 1999 <http://www.worldbookonline.com/na/ar/fs/ar388680.htm>.

Sultzman, Lee. "Delaware History." 23 Nov. 1998. <http://www.dickshovel.com/dela.html>.

Vallis, Glenn. "New Jersey During the Revolution." 13 Sept. 1998. <http://www.eclipse.net/~gvalis/ggv/NJrev/NJrev.html>.

Arnett, Bill. "Saturn." *The Nine Planets.* 21 May 1998. <http://seds.lpl.arizona.edu/nineplanets/nineplanets/saturn.html>.

"Discovering Whales." *Welcome to the Watery World of Whales.*

14 Oct. 1998. <http://whales.magna.com.au/DISCOVER/index.html>.

8 Appendices

Works Cited for Grades 5 and 6

1. For each source listed, begin first line at margin and indent each line that follows.
2. Underline or use italics for titles of books, periodicals and software. Titles of articles are enclosed in quotation marks.
3. Note punctuation and follow exactly.
4. If required information, such as author or place of publication, is not available, just leave it out.
5. Arrange all sources in one list, alphabetically by first word, which will generally be either the author's last name or the first important word of the title.

PRINT SOURCES

Book with one author:

1. Author.
2. *Title of book.* (italicized)
3. City of publication:
4. Publisher, date of publication.

Cohen, Daniel. *America's Very Own Ghosts.* New York: Doubleday, 1985.

Book with two authors:

1. Authors (in the order they are given in the book).
2. *Title of book.* (italicized)
3. City of publication:
4. Publisher, date.

Smith, Elizabeth, and David Wright. *Rocks and Minerals.* Chicago: Macmillan, 1995.

Encyclopedia and other familiar reference books:

1. Author of article (if available).
2. "Title of article."
3. *Title of book.* (italicized)

8 Appendices

4. Date of edition. (Volume and page number not necessary if articles are arranged alphabetically).

   Eiselen, Malcolm R. "Franklin, Benjamin." *The World Book Encyclopedia.* 1999.

   "France." *Compton's Encyclopedia.* 1998.

Article in a periodical:
1. Author (if available).
2. "Title of article."
3. *Periodical title* (italicized) date: page.

   Haverkamp, Beth. "Bad Women and Bandit Queens." *Cobblestone* May 1996: 20-22.

   "N.F.L. Training Camp Report" *The New York Times* 21 Aug. 1996: B12.

INTERVIEW CONDUCTED BY THE RESEARCHER
1. Name of person interviewed.
2. Type of interview.
3. Date of interview.

   Whitman, Christie. Personal interview. 20 Aug. 1999.

   Ford, Harrison. Telephone interview. 26 Jan. 1999.

ELECTRONIC SOURCES

Encyclopedia and other publications on CD-ROM:
1. Author (if available).
2. "Title of article."
3. *Title of product* (italicized or in italics).
4. Edition or version (if relevant)
5. CD-ROM.
6. City of publication: Publisher, date of publication.

   Cashman, Katharine V. "Volcano." *World Book Multimedia Encyclopedia.* 1999 ed. CD-ROM. Chicago: World Book Inc., 1999.

   "Japan." *Cartopedia.* CD-ROM. New York: Dorling Kindersley, 1995.

8 Appendices

Solnick, Bruce B. "Columbus, Christopher." *Grolier MultiMedia Encyclopedia.* 1994 ed. CD-ROM. Danbury, CT: Grolier Electronic Publishing, Inc., 1992.

Leicester, Henry M. "Chemistry." *Microsoft Encarta.* 1998 ed. CD-ROM. Redmond, WA: Microsoft Corporation, 1998.

"Engine, Four-Stroke." *David Macauley: The Way Things Work.* CD-ROM. New York: Dorling Kindersley, 1994.

Periodical article found in CD-ROM database:

1. Author.
2. "Title of article."
3. *Periodical title* (italicized) date: page.
4. *Title of database.* (italicized)
5. CD- ROM.
6. City of publication: name of electronic publisher, date of electronic publication.

   Gray, Robert. "Do You Believe in Dragons?" *Ranger Rick* Oct 1993: 21-29. SIRS Discoverer. CD-ROM. Boca Raton: SIRS, Inc., Spring 1996.

   Timney, Mark C. "Virtual Chills and Thrills." *Boys' Life* April 1995: 13-15. Primary Search. CD-ROM. Peabody, MA: Ebsco, Mar. 1996.

ONLINE SOURCES

Encyclopedia from an online service:

1. Author, if shown
2. "Title of the article."
3. *Name of encyclopedia* (italicized).
4. Name of publisher, date of publication, if available.
5. Date of your visit.
6. Name of the online subscription service hosting the encyclopedia..

   "Animal Rights." *Compton's Living Encyclopedia.* Compton's Learning Company, 1996. 22 Aug. 1999. America Online.

   Ketcham, Ralph. "Franklin, Benjamin." *Grolier Multimedia Encyclopedia.* Grolier Interactive Inc. 10 Sept. 1999. CLAMSnet.

8 Appendices

Periodical article from an online database:

1. Author.
2. "Title of article."
3. *Periodical title* (italicized) date: page.
4. *Name of database.* (italicized)
5. Publisher of database (if available).
6. Date of visit.
7. <http address>. (enclosed in angle brackets)

Peterson, Robert W. "Teddy Roosevelt: The Conservation President." *Boys' Life* April 1994: 28. *Primary Search.* EBSCO Publishing. 12 Nov. 2000. <http://ebsco.com/primary>.

World Wide Web:

1. Author (if known).
2. "Title of article."
3. *Title of complete work.* (if relevant, italicized)
4. Date of visit.
5. <full http address>. (enclosed in angle brackets)

Boritt, Gabor S. "Civil War." *World Book Online.* 10 September 1999. <http://www.worldbookonline.com/na/ar/fs/ar117060.htm>.

Norton, R.J. "An Overview of John Wilkes Booth's Assassination of President Abraham Lincoln." *Abraham Lincoln's Assassination* 28 Nov. 1999. <http://home.att.net/~rjnorton/Lincoln75.html>.

"Statistical Summary: America's Major Wars." *The U.S. Civil War Center.* 14 Aug. 1999. <http://www.cwc.lsu.edu/other/stats/warcost.htm>.

Arnett, Bill. "Callisto." *The Nine Planets.* 21 May 1999. <http://seds.lpl.arizona.edu/nineplanets/nineplanets/callisto.html>.

Winter, Mark. "Nitrogen." *WebElements.* 9 July 1999. <http://www.shef.ac.uk/chemistry/web-elements/N/key.html>.

8 Appendices

Personal e-mail:

1. Author.
2. "Subject line from posting."
3. Date of posting.
4. Personal e-mail.
5. Date of access.

   Thompson, Barry. "Computer Viruses." 26 Nov. 1999. Personal e-mail. 12 Mar. 2002.

   Bibliographic citation formats developed by Susan Aroldi, aroldi@intac.com, and adapted by Kathy Schrock, kathy@kathyschrock.net.

8 Appendices

Standards for Citations

Citation styles vary in each of the major citation formats, whether they be MLA, APA, Turabian, or the Chicago Manual of Style. Most schools use the MLA format, and samples are listed below. More citation formats can be found in the Nauset Public Schools Research and Style Manual. **(http://www.teachercreated.com/books/3880)**

Web Pages

Format:

Author (if known). "Title of page or document." *Title of site or larger work* (if applicable). Name of editor, compiler, or translator (if any). Publication information for any print version of the source. Date of electronic publication, last update, or date of posting. Name of any associated institution. Date of access.

Example:

"Case History: Anorexia Nervosa." *AMA Health Insight.* 30 Oct. 1998. American Medical Association. 10 Dec. 1999 <http://ama.org/anorexia>.

Newsgroup Postings and Electronic Mail

Format

Sender's Last Name, First Name. "Subject Line from Posting." Day Month Year of Posting. Personal e-mail. (or E-mail to: recipient's name) Day Month Year of Access.

Example:

Smith, William. "Trial results." 12 Jan. 1999. E-mail to John Henry. 29 May 1999.

8 Appendices

Book with one author

Format:

Author last name, first name. *Title of Book.* Place of Publication: Publisher, Date of publication.

Example:

Schrock, Kathleen. *Evaluating Internet Web Sites: An Educator's Guide.* Manhattan, KS: The Master Teacher, 1997.

Book with two or three authors

List the names in the order in which they appear on the title page. Only the first author's name should be reversed. Use a comma between the authors' names. If the persons named on the title page are editors, add a comma after the final name and then the abbreviation "eds."

Format:

Author 1 last name, first name and author 2 first name last name. *Title of book.* Edition (if other than first). Place of publication: Publisher, date of publication.

Example:

Simpson, Carol, and Sharron L. McElmeel. *Internet for Schools.* 2nd ed. Worthington, OH: Linworth Publishing, 1997.

Encyclopedias and Reference Books

Format:

Author of Article. "Article Title." *Title of Reference Book.* Place of Publication: Publisher, Date.

Example:

Johnson, Lois. "Pyramid." World Book Encyclopedia. Chicago, IL: World Book, 1992.

Appendices

Periodical

Abbreviate the months. Dates for weekly or bi-weekly magazines should be written in this order: Day Month Year.

If the article is on consecutive pages, note the page numbers of the entire article, e.g., 16–20. If the article is not on consecutive pages write only the first page number followed by a plus sign: 27+.

Format:

Author last name, first name. "Title of article." *Periodical title* Month Year: pages.

Example:

Ramsey, Pamela. "Where's My Smiley Face?" *MacWorld* Sept.1997: 86-92+.

CD-ROM

Format:

Author's Name. "Article Title." *CD ROM Title.* Edition. CD-ROM. Place of publication: Publisher, Year.

Example:

Cashman, Katharine V. "Volcano." *World Book Multimedia Encyclopedia.* 1995 ed. CD-ROM. Chicago: World Book Inc., 1995.

Periodical Article Found in CD-ROM Database

Format:

Author. "Title of article." *Periodical title.* Date of article: Pages. Database source. CD-ROM. Place of publication: Publisher, Date of database.

Example:

Gray, Robert. "Do You Believe in Dragons?" *Ranger Rick.* Oct 1993: 21–29. *SIRS Discoverer.* CD-ROM. Boca Raton: SIRS, Inc., Spring 1996.

8 Appendices

Technology Resources

All of these sites are taken from Kathy Schrock's Guide for Educators at **http://discoveryschool.com/schrockguide/**

Educational Portals

About.com : Elementary Education Resources

...a list of sites in various categories to support the elementary education teacher; includes time management, pen pals, and much more

About.com: Secondary School Resources

...a well-chosen list of resources and topics for secondary school educators and administrators

Awesome Library for Teachers, Students, and Parents

...a nicely arranged, lengthy list of excellent curriculum support sites

Blue Web'n

...a site with critically rated educational links arranged by subject

Appendices

Educational Portals *(cont.)*

Education Index

...a huge directory of sites organized by subject and briefly annotated

Education World

...links to lengthy lists of educational pages; searchable by topic and grade level

42eXplore

...definitions, activities, 4 good starting points, links and resources for over 150 thematic topics

700+ Great Sites

...a wealth of links for kids, teachers, and parents from the ALSC chapter of ALA

8 Appendices

About School Web Pages and the Internet

Acceptable Use Policies—A Handbook

...a well-done overview of the creation of an AUP including links to pages containing components, samples, and templates

A Beginner's Guide to the Internet for Educators

...a well-done tutorial for educators including linked sites and rationale for using the Net in the classroom

Finding Information on the Internet : A Tutorial

...a well-done introduction to the Internet including search strategies

Help Web : A Guide to Getting Started on the Internet

...a nice tutorial on basic Internet use, searching, and links to helpful sites

Appendices

Computer Technology Sites

Butte County Technology Matrix

...a frames-based set of standards to help ensure that "technology integration is evident in curriculum planning, delivery, and evaluation"

California Learning Resource Network: Search the Database

...although created for California teachers, this site provides "a one-stop information source that enables educators to identify supplemental electronic learning resources that both meet local instructional needs and embody the implementation" of content standards

Keyboarding Resources

...handouts, assessments, links for parents and much more information on computer keyboarding

Learning and Teaching Computer Technology Skills in Context

...a great research article, updated in 2002, written by Mike Eisenberg and Doug Johnson, supporting the rationale for infusing technology skills as part of the regular curriculum

National Educational Technology Standards for Students (NETS*S)

...the important document outlining the technology standards for students in grades K-12

8   Appendices

Assessment and the Web

Designing Performance Assessments

...a wealth of information and templates for designing performance assessment tasks for your students

Kathy Schrock's Guide for Educators: Assessment Page

...lists of rubrics, assessment tools, articles, and even report card comments

RubiStar

...an online tool to help the teacher who wants to use rubrics but does not have the time to develop them from scratch; provides the user with a rubric bank which can be edited to meet specific needs

Rubric Builder

...build your own rubric or search the databank for one that you can use or edit

8 Appendices

Online Lesson/Unit Creation Sites

Filamentality

…a online hotlist and instructional tool creation site with lots of guidance and support throughout the process

Links Builder

…create an online annotated hotlist of sites for students to use in support of a unit or lesson

TrackStar

...an awesome series of Internet integration curriculum units; use one of these or create your own

WebQuest Page

...a site which provides descriptions and examples of how to use this great model of Internet integration in the classroom

8 Appendices

HTML: The Next Step

If you've read this far in the book, you already know the World Wide Web is a dynamic place. Pages appear and disappear on the whim of their creators; links accumulate, change, or are deleted without notice; and entire sites are seemingly swallowed up, erased like the lost continent of Atlantis. Hopefully, after reading this book, you have the skills to be able to search the Web and also scour the educational portals to find the sites you need.

There is, however another aspect of change on the Web that needs to be addressed. Every so often, the World Wide Web Consortium, affectionately referred to as the W3C, releases a series of recommendations dealing with the way Web browsers should display the information on a Web page. These changes are thought out very carefully over a period of months and are taken very seriously by Web page designers and the producers of graphical browsers. In the past, some of these proposed changes were radical; for instance, the introduction of tables and frames produced quite an uproar. The appropriateness (and legality) of using frames is still hotly debated. Some of the newer recommendations include standards for Cascading Style Sheets, DHTML, and XML, all of which take advantage of new technologies to create more interactive Web pages.

The good news is that nothing changes over night. The latest versions of both *Netscape* and *Internet Explorer* already support some of the proposed changes. However, by the time all of the new methods of Web page creation are adopted by these two browser giants, the W3C will be hard at work creating a new set of proposed changes in some other area.

Even better news is that methods of page creation and HTML tags and rules currently in place are almost always backwards compatible. The official term used by the W3C for HTML tags and constructs when they are phased out is "deprecated." They use this term to indicate that people responsible for creating Web pages ought to use the new methods instead of the old ones.

8 Appendices

What can you do to stay abreast of these changes? When you purchase an upgrade to an HTML editor such as *HomeSite* or *Dreamweaver*, the newest tags and features are already built in. The software usually contains an explanation of all of these new additions and their impact on page design. You also could visit the W3C site and read about the modifications slated for the next version of HTML. Be warned that this is not light reading! However, after completing this book and publishing your own Web pages following the outline provided in the preceding pages, you may be up to the challenge!

9 Glossary of Terms

attribute

an addition to an HTML tag that informs the browser to do something additional to a standard tag (border=0, align=right)

bookmark

an electronic list of places you have visited on the Web and want to remember (This is done with your browser and may be called a "favorite." The browser remembers these URLs for you.)

browser

a software program which translates HTML pages and makes them appear as organized graphics and text on your screen (*Netscape Navigator, Internet Explorer*, etc.)

case sensitive

distinguishing between capital and lowercase letters. (Browsers read in a case sensitive format, and all file names must be referenced exactly the way they are named.)

center

place in a classroom where teams of students (2 or 3) are assigned for a period of time to accomplish a task (Teams are rotated through these areas so that all students have access to the activity.)

convert

to change from one program or format to another

crop

cutting the size of a graphic by drawing a box around the part which you want to see and selecting "crop" or "trim" from the edit menu bar while in a graphics program or graphic converter

9 Glossary of Terms

document source

the HTML coding and text information of a page on the Web (The document source code can be viewed by holding down the "view source" menu item on your browser toolbar and then highlighting document source. The source is written and saved in a text format.)

download

to bring digital information on to your computer

e–mail

electronic mail, an online Internet protocol for sending messages over the Internet that is almost instantaneous

FTP

File Transfer Protocol

the process of sending documents and graphics electronically out to a server so they can be viewed on the World Wide Web

home page

opening home page for a school or class

GIF

"Graphic Interchange Format," a format used to display line-drawn graphics on the Internet (pronounced with a hard G)

graphic converter

a program to change the format of a document from one type to another, for example, converting a PICT graphic document created in a drawing program to a GIF file so it can be viewed on the Internet

9 Glossary of Terms

hard copies

paper copies of information which you print out, original artwork done by students, or original photographs

home page

the first page in any Web site

HTML

Hypertext Markup Language, the code or language used to write Web pages; HTML is read by your browser to determine how to display the graphics and text on a Web page

hypertext links

highlighted words on a Web page which, when selected, take you to another place on the site page or to another site

IP

Internet protocol, one of the important rules which govern how information travels over the Internet

JPEG or JPG

Joint Photographic Experts Group

a format for saving digital photographs which allows graphics to be shown on Internet browsers and keeps the file size small by compressing it

listserv

mailing lists which send simultaneously send the same e-mail message to any subscribed members of the list

9 Glossary of Terms

load time

the amount of time it takes to download a complete Web page to your browser which can be affected by the speed and type of your connection as well as the number and document size of graphics which are loading on the page

local expert

onsite teacher/specialist who can help with all the computer and Internet questions which arise every day

lurking

reading the posted information in a newsgroup for a time before posting a message

memory-heavy (memory-intensive)

any large file which loads slowly on your Web page

mentor

a person or a process (mentoring) for sharing and teaching information on a new topic

netiquette

the accepted rules (etiquette) for using the Web; i.e. you should never write e-mail in all capital letters since this is analogous to shouting

newbie

a person just beginning to use the Web, e-mail, or any new computer program

newsgroup

a subject-specific, bulletin board-like posting of questions, answers, and ideas; unlike a listserv, the postings are stored in a central location and they are not delivered to your e-mail box

9 Glossary of Terms

PICT

the format with which many Macintosh word processing programs save graphics and which has to be changed to use the graphic on the Internet

pixel

the smallest element that makes up a graphic image, which is measured in pixel height and pixel width

PNG

Portable Network Graphics

an additional image file format which combines some of the best features from both the GIF and the JPEG format; is supported by the major browsers

post(see also FTP)

the process of sending documents and graphics electronically out to a server so they can be viewed on the World Wide Web

scan

to use a scanner to convert a paper or "real" document to a digital format

9 Glossary of Terms

scanner

a device which takes a digital picture of a hard copy and records it as a digital file; the image may then be adjusted, rotated, and cropped

source code

the HTML text and tags which tell the browser how to display the Web page; it determines the size a graphic is shown, links to other pages, size of text, and location of everything on the Web page

storyboard

method of brainstorming lots of ideas and then organizing them

tags

text, numbers, and brackets which are placed around your words and graphics in the HTML source code to tell the browser how to display the information

teachable moment

that perfect unplanned, time to teach a specific topic

template

a Web page which displays a sample format for a page; designed for others to adapt as their own; it includes the coding already

9 Glossary of Terms

upload

sending information from your computer to a network or other source

URL (Uniform Resource Locator)

this is the Web address that you type into the location bar on the browser

user-friendly

something which is designed to be easily used with little effort or training

wait time

the time the viewer spends waiting for a page of information to load on the Web

10 Bibliography of Books and Resources

Anderson, Mary Alice. "Developing Web Page Policies or Guidelines." *Technology Connection.* May-June 1997.

Gilster, Paul. *Digital Literacy.* New York: Wiley, 1997.

Harris, Judy. *Virtual Architecture: Designing and Directing Curriculum-Based Telecomputing.* Oregon: ISTE, 1997.

Kobler, Ron, ed. *The Illustrated Book of Terms and Technology.* Lincoln, NE: Sandhills Publishing, 1998.

Lemay, Laura. *Teach Yourself Web Publishing with HTML and XHTML in 21 Days.* 3d. ed. Indianapolis, IN: Sams.net, 2001.

McKenzie, Jamieson. *Home Sweet Home: Creating Web Pages That Deliver.* 1996. 2 November 2002. <http://fno.org/homesweet.html>.

March, Tom. *Working the Web for Education.* 2001. 2 November 2002. <http://www.ozline.com/learning/theory.html>.

Schrock, Kathleen. *Evaluating Internet Web Sites: An Educator's Guide.* Manhattan, KS: The Master Teacher, 1997.

Schrock, Kathleen. *Research and Style Manual.*

Templeton, Brad. *10 Big Myths About Copyright Explained.* n.d. 2 November 2002. <http://www.templetons.com/brad//copymyths.html>.

Notes